D0722331

UNDERSTANDING
JAMAICA KINCAID

Understanding Contemporary American Literature
Matthew J. Bruccoli, Series Editor

Volumes on

Edward Albee • Sherman Alexie • Nicholson Baker
John Barth • Donald Barthelme
The Beats • The Black Mountain Poets • Robert Bly
Raymond Carver • Fred Chappell • Chicano Literature
Contemporary American Drama
Contemporary American Horror Fiction
Contemporary American Literary Theory
Contemporary American Science Fiction, 1926–1970
Contemporary American Science Fiction, 1970–2000
Contemporary Chicana Literature
Robert Coover • James Dickey • E. L. Doctorow • Rita Dove
John Gardner • George Garrett • John Hawkes • Joseph Heller
Lillian Hellman • Beth Henley • John Irving
Randall Jarrell • Charles Johnson • Adrienne Kennedy
William Kennedy • Jack Kerouac • Jamaica Kincaid
Ursula K. Le Guin • Denise Levertov • Bernard Malamud
Bobbie Ann Mason • Jill McCorkle • Carson McCullers
W. S. Merwin • Arthur Miller • Toni Morrison's Fiction
Vladimir Nabokov • Gloria Naylor • Joyce Carol Oates
Tim O'Brien • Flannery O'Connor • Cynthia Ozick
Walker Percy • Katherine Anne Porter • Richard Powers
Reynolds Price • Annie Proulx • Thomas Pynchon
Theodore Roethke • Philip Roth • May Sarton • Hubert Selby, Jr.
Mary Lee Settle • Neil Simon • Isaac Bashevis Singer
Jane Smiley • Gary Snyder • William Stafford
Anne Tyler • Kurt Vonnegut • David Foster Wallace
Robert Penn Warren • James Welch • Eudora Welty
Tennessee Williams • August Wilson

UNDERSTANDING
JAMAICA
KINCAID

Justin D. Edwards

The University of South Carolina Press

© 2007 University of South Carolina

Published by the University of South Carolina Press
Columbia, South Carolina 29208

www.sc.edu/uscpress

Manufactured in the United States of America

16 15 14 13 12 11 10 09 08 07   10 9 8 7 6 5 4 3 2 1

Library of Congress Cataloging-in-Publication Data

Edwards, Justin D., 1970–
    Understanding Jamaica Kincaid / Justin D. Edwards.
        p. cm. — (Understanding contemporary American literature)
    Includes bibliographical references and index.
    ISBN-13: 978-1-57003-688-0 (cloth : alk. paper)
    ISBN-10: 1-57003-688-8 (cloth : alk. paper)
    1. Kincaid, Jamaica—Criticism and interpretation. I. Title.
    PR9275.A583K56435 2007
    813'.54—dc22

                                                    2006038765

Contents

Series Editor's Preface

The volumes of *Understanding Contemporary American Literature* have been planned as guides or companions for students as well as good nonacademic readers. The editor and publisher perceive a need for these volumes because much of the influential contemporary literature makes special demands. Uninitiated readers encounter difficulty in approaching works that depart from the traditional forms and techniques of prose and poetry. Literature relies on conventions, but the conventions keep evolving; new writers form their own conventions—which in time may become familiar. Put simply, *UCAL* provides instruction in how to read certain contemporary writers—identifying and explicating their material, themes, use of language, point of view, structures, symbolism, and responses to experience.

The word *understanding* in the titles was deliberately chosen. Many willing readers lack an adequate understanding of how contemporary literature works; that is, what the author is attempting to express and the means by which it is conveyed. Although the criticism and analysis in the series have been aimed at a level of general accessibility, these introductory volumes are meant to be applied in conjunction with the works they cover. They do not provide a substitute for the works and authors they introduce, but rather prepare the reader for more profitable literary experiences.

M. J. B.

CHAPTER 1

Understanding Jamaica Kincaid

Jamaica Kincaid achieved fame as a writer of fiction in 1983 when her first book, a collection of short stories titled *At the Bottom of the River,* was published to wide critical acclaim. That collection launched her career as a force in contemporary American literature: it won the Morton Dauwen Zabel Award and the American Academy and Institute of Letters Prize. More honors followed for her second book, a novel titled *Annie John* (1985), which was a finalist for the international Ritz Paris Hemingway Award and which was widely and favorably reviewed by critics, who generally described the novel as poetic, emotional, and direct.[1] In 1989 she was the recipient of a Guggenheim fellowship, and in 1991 she received honorary degrees from Williams College and Long Island University. With the publication of *The Autobiography of My Mother* in 1997, Kincaid won the Lannan Literary Award. This established her place as an important contemporary writer and paved the way for her election to the American Academy of Arts and Letters in 2004. Kincaid had been writing pieces for the *New Yorker* long before the publication of her first book. As early as 1974, she wrote an article called "West Indian Weekend," which was the first of eighty-five unsigned "Talk of the Town" pieces to be written for the *New Yorker* over a period of ten years. In 1976 she was appointed as a staff writer for the *New Yorker,* where her gardening column appeared regularly until 1996. In all of her early writings, Kincaid developed a distinctive prose style, combining complex poetic abstractions with fluid and direct language.

The daughter of Annie Richardson and Frederick Potter, Jamaica Kincaid was born in St. John's, Antigua, on May 25, 1949. Soon after her birth her parents gave her the name Elaine Potter Richardson, but she decided to change her name legally to Jamaica Kincaid in 1973. Changing her name was, as Kincaid says, a liberation that gave her the freedom to write whatever she wanted. She also states that she chose this name because it reflected her complex identity as a Caribbean woman who was marked by a British colonial education system. The name of the island of Jamaica is, after all, an English corruption of what Columbus called "Xaymaca," and "Kincaid" is a common surname throughout the English-speaking world. The combination of the two names, then, provided her a new identity for her new life in the United States. But it was also a name that connected her to her roots in the Caribbean and her colonial past. This process of renaming is a theme that appears throughout Kincaid's works, for renaming is often used as a metaphor for conquest and colonial domination.

Kincaid's mother, Annie Drew, was born in Dominica, and she moved to Antigua when she was a young woman. Annie appears in many of Kincaid's fiction and nonfiction writings; she is often referred to as a loving, and yet stifling, maternal figure, as well as a dedicated homemaker, gardener, and a political activist. Kincaid's biological father was an Antiguan taxi driver who abandoned his wife and children. He is the subject of the novel *Mr. Potter* (2002), wherein Kincaid describes the father she did not know. When Kincaid was very young, her mother was remarried to a man named David Drew. Her biological father did not play a significant role in her childhood, while her stepfather, a cabinetmaker and carpenter, was the man she called her father.

At the age of three, Kincaid was taught to read by her mother, and she was also enrolled in the Moravian School. While a child, she also attended the Antiguan Girls School and the Princess Margaret School before being apprenticed to a seamstress. In 1958, when Kincaid was nine, her mother gave birth to Joseph Drew, the first of Kincaid's three brothers. After the birth of Joseph, Kincaid's mother shifted her attention away from her daughter, focusing her efforts on the raising of her male child. It was around this time that Kincaid also began to be critical of her native island. Both of these events gave rise to two of the central themes in her fiction: the inequality of gender relations and the aftermath of colonization. At an early age, Kincaid recognized that daughters were treated very differently from sons and that Antigua had been severely scarred by its history of British imperial rule. She thus began to criticize gender hierarchies, as well as those colonized subjects who had internalized the views and ideologies of the colonial power. As a result, she began to question her education: an education that was tainted by gender divisions and narratives passed down by the British—narratives that ignored the Antiguan history of slavery and subjugation. Her critical mind and analytical eye meant that she became identified as a troublemaker by her teachers.[2]

During interviews Kincaid often speaks of her youth as marked by hardships and losses, but she also describes moments of peace and harmony in a place that sometimes offered her a sense of tranquility and spiritual fulfilment. At the same time, though, what shines through in most of her writing is a depiction of the small attitudes and oppressive atmospheres that encompassed her childhood on Antigua. Indeed the sunshine, warmth, and picturesque surroundings found in her depictions of the island are usually offset by the images of imprisonment and suffocation in this "small place." A frequent theme of Kincaid's fiction is the way that this ten-by-twelve-mile island traps its citizens and discourages them from reflecting upon their experiences, analyzing their situations, or controlling their destinies. Antigua is, Kincaid states, a kind of prison.

In 1965, shortly following her sixteenth birthday, Kincaid left Antigua for the United States. Her first job in her adopted country was as an au pair in Scarsdale, New York. In her article, "Jamaica Kincaid's New York," she describes her first American employers as sympathetic and generous people who, while somewhat patronizing, gave her the freedom to explore the exciting urban world of New York City: "That was the first thing I wanted to do," Kincaid writes about her arrival in Scarsdale, "take the train to New York."[3] In fact, her attraction to the city would remain a significant factor throughout her youth, inspiring her to leave her job in Scarsdale for a position as an au pair with a wealthy family on the Upper East Side of Manhattan. At this time she also found it important to continue her education, and soon after immigrating she began to take classes at Westchester Community College in White Plains, New York, and then later at Franconia College in Franconia, New Hampshire. Her interest in the visual arts also led her to take photography classes at the New School for Social Research, but ultimately she was drawn into the publishing world when she found a job with *Art Direction* magazine.

She was fired from *Art Direction* for writing a controversial article on black American advertising.[4] The political commitment and confrontational style that marks her later writing is shown in this early piece. Kincaid has never shied away from expressing her views even if those views will make others angry and result in opposition or protest. She then did a series of successful articles for *Ingenue* magazine in which she interviewed celebrities and asked them what they were like between the ages of fifteen and seventeen. Kincaid refers to these articles as the texts that began her writing career.

After choosing a new career in a new country, she also chose a new name. In 1973, at the age of twenty-four, Elaine Potter Richardson became Jamaica Kincaid. She has accounted for this change in three ways. First, it established a distance between her and her family, giving her the anonymity needed to adopt intensely personal material for her writing (such as the recurring theme of the love-hate relationship between mother and daughter). Second, her chosen name identified her with a specific region of the Americas—a region marked by exploitation and the violent history of slavery (another important theme in her writing). Third, it marked a transformation from an old sense of self to a new identity (a theme that is explored in all of her novels). Just as Frederick Douglass recognized the importance of taking on a new name at the end of his slave narrative, Kincaid writes that, for her, the process of being named by someone else was a mark of possession and ownership. Conversely, the naming of oneself is a powerful assertion of agency, freedom, and liberation.[5]

In September 1974 the *New Yorker* published Kincaid's first "Talk of the Town" article. This piece was in fact a series of notes that William Shawn—then the editor of the magazine—decided to print without telling Kincaid. The article is a description of the annual Caribbean carnival held in Brooklyn, but the piece takes a typically autobiographical turn, for Kincaid uses the event to write about her relationship to her mother. These kinds of autobiographical references are also present in some of her other "Talk of the Town" articles: at times she refers to her education in Antigua, at other times she refers to her father, and sometimes she even comments on her life in Manhattan. Not all of these pieces draw on personal experiences, but many of them include autobiographical content that Kincaid also explores in her major novels.

Kincaid's first work of fiction, a short story titled "Girl," appeared in the *New Yorker* in 1977. Occupying only one page, this single-sentence story is told in a voice that is quite distinct from her earlier journalistic pieces. The voice of "Girl" delves into many layers of discourse, and the story explores the way in which a mother's language can affect the psychological state of her daughter. In fact, the oppressive voice of the mother lies behind the words that seem to be resonating in the head of the child. The story is not composed using the conventions of narrative development or sequential coherence. Instead the reader is presented with a long detailed list of commands and rules that speaks to the internalization of discourse in the mother-daughter dynamic as well as the regulation of specific gender codes of conduct. The voice of the mother holds a commanding presence in the story, suggesting that one is never truly free of the maternal voice and the instructions that pass from mother to daughter.

"Girl" also appeared as the lead story in Kincaid's first book, *At the Bottom of the River* (1983). Some critics were puzzled by the surreal and fragmentary style of this book, but all of the reviews identified Kincaid as offering a unique and refreshing voice. In a review in the *Washington Post,* for instance, Doris Grumbach focused on the originality of Kincaid's voice: "Hers is a voice you have never heard before," Grumbach writes, "exhilarating to read and impossible to forget."[6] Susan Sontag went as far as to say that some of the stories were "thrilling," "sumptuous," and "irresistible," and they constituted some of the best writing in years "by a writer from this continent."[7] And Derek

Walcott said that he read the book with "that soft succession of 'yeses' that we silently give to what Hemingway called 'the true sentence.'"[8]

Kincaid's connection with the *New Yorker* continued to be beneficial for her writing career. After the success of her early journalism and fiction, the magazine published *Annie John* as a series of short stories before its publication in book form in 1985. When *Annie John* appeared in bookstores, it received rave reviews in North America and the United Kingdom. Writing in the *Boston Herald,* Paula Bonnell, for instance, commented on the impressive economy of the prose, stating that "rarely has so much been done in so few pages."[9] Susan Kenney, writing in the *New York Times Book Review,* thought the story so "touching and familiar it could be happening in Anchorage, so inevitable it could be happening to any of us, any time, any place. And that's exactly the book's strength, its wisdom, its truth."[10] The review in the *Washington Post* was representative of the novel's reception, for it focused on Kincaid's commingling of realism and poetic abstraction. The reviewer called the novel "movingly real" with "poetry that is grounded in detail, in the lovingly rendered life of its adolescent heroine."[11]

Kincaid's burgeoning literary success in the 1980s was not impeded by the growth of her family. In 1979 she had married the composer Allen Shawn, who was the son of William Shawn, the *New Yorker* editor. By the time *Annie John* was published, she had given birth to a daughter, Annie, and in 1988 the couple had a son, Harold. Kincaid has spoken about the convergence of her writing and her family life. "I am essentially a person very interested in domestic life," she told Donna Perry in a interview, "and very interested in things that we think of, either in a good or a bad way, as women's things. . . . In fact, I think I reduce

everything to the domestic situation. . . . It's not anything delib-
erate or a statement or anything, that's just how I understand
things."[12]

Understanding things is an important theme in the book that
followed *Annie John. A Small Place* (1988) is a long essay that
offers a candid and powerful account of the island of Kincaid's
youth. It is an expansive work that touches on everything from
the history of colonization to the contemporary American
tourist industry that is essential to the island's economy. Kincaid's third book was not as well received as her first two. Robert
Gottlieb, the editor of the *New Yorker* who replaced Shawn,
refused to publish it because he felt that the essay expressed too
much bitterness and anger. This same criticism was expressed by
several reviewers. A writer for the *New York Times,* for instance,
said that the book was "distorted by [Kincaid's] anger."[13] And a
reviewer for *New Statesman and Society* wrote that Kincaid
"loses control of her material, and inexplicably descends into a
snivelling attack on the sins of the nasty—and long departed—
colonial power."[14] On the other hand, a number of reviews were
extremely positive. Caryl Phillips's review for the *Los Angeles
Times Book Review* heralded the essay's "rich and evocative
prose," calling the book an "urgent and poetic" piece that offered important, yet difficult, truths about the past and present.[15]
And Salmon Rushdie's review of *A Small Place* praised the text
as "a jeremiad of great clarity and force that one might have
called torrential were the language not so finely controlled."[16]

Kincaid returned to fiction in 1990 with the publication of
Lucy. This novel tells the story of a nineteen-year-old West
Indian girl, Lucy, who sheds her cloistered colonial upbringing
for a job as an au pair in New York City. Lucy's developing subjectivity occurs alongside the deterioration of her employers'

marriage, and the eventual divorce of the couple triggers Lucy's memories of family life. In fact, Lucy's search for a sense of belonging leads to her disturbing reflections about the nature of "home" and attempts to establish a new homeland in a foreign country. The novel continues to explore some of the themes found in *A Small Place*—exploitation, colonization, and power relations—but *Lucy* also returns to many of the themes covered in *Annie John*. Indeed *Lucy* picks up where *Annie John* leaves off: the girl has now left her home in Antigua and tries to forge a new life for herself in the United States.

In general, *Lucy* received positive reviews. Many critics were interested in Kincaid's combination of autobiography and fiction, while others applauded her forthright depiction of a West Indian immigrant who tries to create a new life for herself in New York. Other critics saw the novel as a progression in Kincaid's literary growth—a book that built upon the themes first expressed in *Annie John*. Jane Mendelsohn's review in the *Village Voice*, for instance, praised *Lucy* for its "subtle evocation of shifting patterns" and added that the novel "reveals more gradations in quality of possible experience than any of Kincaid's previous work."[17] A reviewer for the *Wall Street Journal* wrote that Lucy "confirms Jamaica Kincaid as both a daughter of Charlotte Bronte and Virginia Woolf," while a writer in *USA Today* stated that the "lyrical simplicity with which she [Kincaid] tells this story makes it enormously moving."[18]

In 1996 Kincaid published another highly autobiographical novel titled *The Autobiography of My Mother*. This book is set in Dominica and depicts the haunting story of Xuela Claudette Richardson, the daughter of a Carib mother and half-Scottish, half-African father. Xuela's mother dies giving birth to her, and her father leaves her to be raised by his laundress. The writing style is similar to Kincaid's earlier work: she combines clear and economical sentences with lyrical phrases that express deeply charged emotions. Like *Annie John* and *Lucy,* this novel is an account of a woman's love, fear, loss, and the forging of subjectivity within an oppressive community that is marked by gender hierarchies, class differences, and a legacy of colonization. In fact, in her review for the *Times Union* of Albany, New York, Margaria Fichtner writes that Xuela is, like Kincaid, "obsessed by conquest, colonialism, class and culture, the clouded process of identity and the travails of stumbling toward adulthood bereft of the sweet cushion of material love."[19] Writing in the *New York Times Book Review,* Cathleen Schine described the book as "pure and overwhelming, a brilliant fable of willed nihilism."[20] And indeed many reviews commented on the bleakness of the novel, pointing out that it contained less hope for the future than Kincaid's earlier fiction.

During the mid-1990s, Kincaid's brother, Devon Drew, suffered from AIDS and eventually died in January of 1996. Devon became the subject of her 1997 memoir, *My Brother,* which recounts the story of Devon's life, illness, and death. Kincaid writes about how she was summoned back to Antigua from Vermont (where she continues to live) and how she experiences conflicting emotions on her visit "home": on the one hand, she wants to forgive the suffering caused by her mother's narcissism and her brother's self-destructiveness, but, on the other hand, she must also distance herself from her pain and her family's power to consume her life. Some reviewers were disappointed by the book. Peter Kurth writing in *Salon,* for instance, called *My Brother* one of the most "overrated books of 1997," and he criticized Kincaid for writing a "bitter diatribe" on her mother rather than a sympathetic portrait of her brother's struggle with

AIDS.[21] Somewhat less harsh was Meredith Maran's review in the *San Francisco Chronicle;* she stated that "despite Kincaid's self-absorbed criticisms of others' self-absorption, there is much brilliant writing and thinking in the pages of *My Brother.*"[22]

Those critics who published negative reviews of *My Brother* tended to criticize the book for focusing too much on the author herself rather than on the tragedy of Devon Drew's disease and premature death. The title is somewhat misleading, for the book is not, in fact, about Kincaid's brother. Instead it is, like her earlier work, a meditation on gender relations, sexuality, power, and motherhood. The bond that ties Kincaid to her brother is simply a springboard from which she dives into other subjects, including the bonds between mothers and daughters, adults and children, men and women, colonizer and colonized.

Kincaid's most recent novel, *Mr. Potter,* appeared in 2002. The text is a speculative piece of fiction about her father—a man whom she did not know. "All I had was his birth certificate, his death certificate and his father's birth certificate to go on," Kincaid told Kim McLarin in an interview, "I didn't know anything about him except that he was a chauffeur."[23] *Mr. Potter* follows the life of an uneducated chauffeur as he works and lives in Antigua. The book is written from the perspective of the narrating daughter who has never had a relationship with her father and who tries to piece together his life through a series of speculations and repetitions. The reception of *Mr. Potter* was generally positive. Jeremy Taylor's article on Kincaid in *Caribbean Beat* calls the novel a powerful and thought-provoking work about an illiterate man "who remains blank, unaware of the rest of the world, without a context for what happens in life."[24] And Adam Mars-Jones's review in the *Observer* stated that the novel was "entertaining and seducing," and he called attention to Kincaid's "bewitching" and Steinian prose style.[25] With this focus on her father, Kincaid once again turned to her family tree for inspiration and material. Kincaid touched on this relationship between her writing and family ties in a recent interview with Kim McLarin: "It is not difficult for me to think about my family or write about them," she said, "because my family makes up a great deal of my literary imagination."[26]

Overall, Kincaid's fiction is concerned with the way an individual conducts her life in the face of social, familial, economic, political, and gendered hierarchies. From *At the Bottom of the River*, with its focus on the complex gender and racial divisions in the Caribbean, to *Annie John*, which expresses the feelings of loss and anger when faced with the disparities between sons and daughters, the author explores power relations in the context of personal identity. Such themes are also treated in *The Autobiography of My Mother*, which depicts the history of a poor, abandoned girl who is able to draw on her sexuality (which is also sometimes used as a weapon against her) to gain status and economic stability with a white man. Taking on the American immigrant narrative in *Lucy*, Kincaid shows how conceptions of gender and racial divisions can influence the life of the individual in the United States. And in *Mr. Potter* she offers the portrait of a philandering man from the perspective of an abandoned daughter who never knew her father.

Ever since the publication of *The Autobiography of My Mother*—a novel about a woman who obsessively tries to weave together the history of the mother who died giving birth to her—critics have compared Kincaid's writing to that of Gertrude Stein.[27] After all, *The Autobiography of My Mother* has a formal and stylistic connection to Stein's *Autobiography of Alice B. Toklas* (1933), a text in which Stein plays with the generic conventions of the autobiography and mixes together fact and fiction. The repetitive style of *Mr. Potter* has also been compared to the repetition that Stein cultivated in her literary "portraits" of modernist artists such as Pablo Picasso and T. S. Eliot. In his review of *Mr. Potter,* for instance, Adam Mars-Jones writes that Kincaid has "venture[d] into the parlour of modernism and pick[ed] up Gertrude Stein's abandoned knitting."[28]

Kincaid's writing has also been likened to Toni Morrison's fiction. This is because both writers tell of the importance of understanding history, particularly a past that is marked by colonization and slavery. Both writers also develop psychologically complicated protagonists who are meant to spark intense emotions in the reader. But most important, both writers recognize the importance of depicting racial difference alongside gender distinctions. Kincaid is, like Morrison, a writer who cannot be clearly delineated as either a black writer or a feminist writer. She is both, and her literary sensibility does not allow one of these identities to take precedence over the other. Kincaid, then, is similar to Morrison in that she is not limited by the large theme of racism, but her texts express an understanding that racial inequities must be comprehended alongside other aspects of subjectivity such as gender and class.[29]

The only conventional autobiographical works by Kincaid are *My Brother,* some of her material on gardening, her travel writing, and a few pieces that she wrote for the *New Yorker.* However, it is clear that Kincaid's novels and short stories, when compared with the narratives she tells about herself in interviews, are based on her childhood experiences in Antigua and her adult life in the United States. Life and fiction merge in her writing, and thus her work is intensely personal. "To speak to me," she says, "is really to read my books. I don't know why I write sometimes, because if you just sat down I would tell you everything in them."[30] Moreover, Kincaid asserts that all of her writing is always, in some sense, autobiographical. "I am driven to write," she says, "so it has to be autobiographical. . . . I'm not interested in things for their own sake. I'm only interested in explaining something for myself. . . . But what I write is also fiction. It wouldn't hold up in a court of law."[31]

Almost all of Kincaid's novels and short stories are first-person narratives. Her fiction thus delves into the emotional and psychological state of the narrator—someone who expresses a subjective perspective on the world. As the narrator tells her story, the text usually proceeds in a linear fashion, but memories and important events from the past, as well as further information about episodes that have occurred in the narrator's life, are revealed as they come into her mind. Thus Kincaid's stories tend to be both chronological and thematic: her texts follow the development of a narrator's life while at the same time returning to common themes such as power, death, loss, mourning, and the haunting presence of history. Her narrators are also extremely self-reflexive, and they constantly comment on the actions that happen around them, usually in precise and powerful language that is thoughtful and poetic.

From this perspective, Kincaid's writing can be read as a cycle of autobiographical and putatively fictional writings that explore her complicated relations with her family in an attempt to work through the problematics of a personal, literary, and historical identity. All of her texts represent a series of journeys that are, in the end, circular. They begin and end with the same motif: one must find self-empowerment through the rejection of ancestry and antecedents while simultaneously recognizing that a complete rejection of the past can never be achieved.

CHAPTER 2

Early Stories
At the Bottom of the River

In her "Talk of the Town" pieces for the *New Yorker,* Kincaid had discovered that invention could be just as "truthful" as fact. For in these "real" articles, she had invented dialogue, invented characters, rearranged events, and introduced herself as a third-person character. In her early fiction, she decided to write about her own life by remolding real events and characters into the short stories that would eventually compose *At the Bottom of the River* (1983). There is very little dialogue in these stories. This allows Kincaid to focus on one point of view in each story, and, as a result, each character usually tells her own story in her own language. The reader is thus given a privileged view of the psychology and emotional state of the first-person narrator. However, these very real voices are occasionally interrupted by voices of authority or by excursions into magic realism, a technique in which a plausible narrative enters the realm of fantasy without establishing a clearly defined line between the possible and the impossible.

The ten stories that make up *At the Bottom of the River* are mostly set in the second half of the twentieth century on the small Caribbean island of Antigua, where great natural beauty exists alongside oppressive social control, poverty, and a history of colonization. Weaving together fact and fiction, these stories capture the sublimity of the surroundings along with the after-effects of personal suffering and trauma. Each text moves from memory to imagination and back again to capture a complex sense of place that is simultaneously attractive and repulsive. Many of the characters and voices presented in the collection live in the moment, but they are haunted, whether they recognize it or not, by a sense of loss that pushes and pulls them in various directions. The themes move from family matters to questions of home and belonging to racial identities and gender distinctions. Each story can be read as an early example of the central materials that constitute Kincaid's later novels: childhood, domesticity, power relations, the mother-daughter bond, personal development, loss, mourning, sensuality, and sexuality. The tone of the writing is highly poetic and heavy with symbolism, for Kincaid presents the reader with numerous voices that articulate complex emotions in a lyrical style.

As in her later fiction, this early work utilizes first-person narration. All of the stories present a distinct voice that tries to come to terms with intricate landscapes that are both internal and external. Taken as a whole, the collection explores the repossession of the self and the assertion of individual independence in the face of the oppressive and stifling love of a mother. Taken individually, each first-person narrator moves from expressing personal pain, anger, mourning, and fear to asserting a sense of strength, hope, determination, and humor.

Drawing on her family as subject matter, Kincaid's early writing anticipates her later work in that she transforms her family history into narratives of loss and defiance. This transformation occurs through speakers who are often not identified, and on a terrain where identities merge together as fantasy blurs with reality. The effect is somewhat surreal and sometimes confusing. The dislocated voices of the texts are fragmentary—echoing modernist experiments with collage—and they offer the reader a slice of life in a specific moment. Some critics found this technique to be very chaotic, and one reviewer even wrote that the book defied sensible communication. Still other critics applauded the text's dreamlike imagery and shifting voices, calling the collection a brilliant, albeit indecipherable, series of dreamscapes.[1]

"Girl"

The first story in the collection, "Girl," is an early example of Kincaid's lyrical and hypnotic tone—a style of writing that uses the rhythms of oral communication to explore the complex layers that make up a character's conscious and subconscious life. One of the most intense stories in the book, "Girl" is a brief fragment, an illuminating flash that contains many of the major themes and issues that Kincaid will develop in her later work. It is about mother-daughter relations, the possibilities and limitations of childhood, the codes of behavior that constitute social control, the regulation of desire, and the restrictions of gender roles. The story presents the voice of a mother instructing her daughter, and the voice seems to echo throughout the mind of the child. The mother is instructive and demanding, but she also constructs a vision of the world that is real for her daughter. In fact, the voice moves from giving advice ("grow okra . . . far from the house because okra tree harbors red ants") to instructions ("this is how you sew on a button") to demands ("don't sing benna in Sunday school") to insults ("walk like a lady and not like the slut you are so bent on becoming").[2]

This short narrative consists of one sentence and begins with the domestic rhythms of everyday life. "Wash the white clothes on Monday and put them on the stone heap; wash the color clothes on Tuesday and put them on the clothesline to dry; don't walk barehead in the sun; cook pumpkin fritters in very hot sweet oil; soak your little cloths right after you take them off" (3). But as the sentence continues, the reader begins to see that the text moves beyond simple domesticity and turns toward larger issues that revolve around the breakdown of binary oppositions. Love blurs into hate as protection becomes destruction, and educational development transforms into the legitimization of regulation as gain turns to loss. "This is how you behave," says the voice of the mother, "in the presence of men who don't know you very well, and this way they won't recognize immediately the slut I have warned you against becoming" (4). Indeed the simplicity of the everyday language becomes a powerful symbol for all of the themes of betrayal and loss that take place on the ground that divides the mother from the daughter, the woman from the girl as the voice of the nurturing mother suddenly mutates into a violent attack that leaves behind a deep scar that can never be fully healed.

The title, "Girl," is highly significant. It is, of course, an oral expression of an exasperated mother speaking to her child. As if the mother were to say, "Girl! what are you doing now?!" Or, "Girl! don't do that!" But the "girl" of the title also places the focus of the story on the daughter herself (rather than the mother) and indicates that this story is really from the girl's point of view. This results in a complex narrative process whereby the reader hears the voice of the mother filtered through the perspective of the daughter and sees the damaging effects of the mother's words from the daughter's vantage point. The narrative thus highlights the power of language; the words not only inflict pain, but they also produce lasting scars and have a profound effect upon the psychological state of the child. The mother's words will forever echo in the girl's head. And as the mother's words turn from instruction to insult, the daughter's emotions move from love to hate.

The mother, though, believes that she is doing what is best for her child. She thinks that she is teaching her daughter about the world, instructing her about practical matters and codes of behavior that will help the child live in this environment. Her advice, then, is not without love and nurturing, for she tries to help her child adapt to the reality of an oppressive and restrictive place, a world that is always judgmental and that will define the girl by her actions.

The West Indian poet Derek Walcott wrote that a Kincaid sentence constantly "heads toward its own contradiction."[3] The sentence that makes up "Girl" is an excellent illustration of Walcott's statement. Contradictions arise in the confusing signals that are communicated to the girl. The mother not only moves from nurturing words to expressions of attack, but she also disrupts clear communication on issues of gender and sexuality. On the one hand, she warns her daughter against becoming a slut ("walk like a lady and not like a slut"; 3). But on the other hand, she instructs her daughter about how to perform an abortion on herself ("this is how to make a good medicine to throw away a child before it even becomes a child"; 5). Moreover, as she repeats the phrase "the slut I know you are so bent on becoming," the mother expresses a sense of inevitability concerning her daughter's rebellion against the gender and sexual rules that she utters (3, 4). A contradiction thus arises through the juxtaposition of the mother's instructions and the simultaneous recognition that the girl will never live up to the social codes of behavior that the mother is trying to teach. As a result, the story ends without ever achieving resolution; instead, contradictions are held in suspension.

This suspension captures the situation of the girl in the story. She is trapped in this world—a world dominated by the all-powerful voice of a mother from whom she cannot escape. After all, the maternal voice is both mesmerizing and paralyzing. It fixes the girl within a specific position from which she can only utter minor protests ("but I don't sing benna on Sundays"; 4). The situation is clear: in order for the girl to develop and grow as an individual she must escape from the oppressive world of her mother. Escape is the only way for her to empower herself. Otherwise, she will not develop or mature, and she will never be able to find her own voice.

"In the Night"

The second story of the collection, "In the Night," is very different from "Girl." Here Kincaid departs from the realism of the first story and enters the dreamlike world of nighttime visions and hallucinations. This story draws on the traditions of surrealism and magic realism to depict a world that is lawless and irrational. Logic has no place here. The reader enters into a realm of obeah magic where mysterious powers take precedence. Conventional notions of time and space—notions associated with modernity—have given way to a darkness that has engulfed enlightenment. The story follows the dreams of a girl who has bizarre visions of "a woman who has removed her skin" and of marrying "a red-skin woman with black bramblebush hair and brown eyes" (6, 11). As one surreal image melts into another, the reader is shown a world of mysterious forces that are never explained. If "Girl" identifies power with the voice of the mother, "In the Night" points to a source of power that lies beyond any particular individual.

The first section of the story is a rejection of rationality. The borders and boundaries separating life from death, the living from the dead, have fallen away and the reader comes face to face with walking dead men such as Mr. Gishard. He has returned to haunt the place where he lived, but he is not a threatening or dangerous figure. Instead he is a harmless ghost who simply wants to gaze at his old home. The women of this section are more threatening, for they are able to use magic to their advantage. The first nameless woman has, for instance, used the darkness to remove her skin and transform herself into a bird. Another woman returns from the dead, but her haunting presence is less innocent than that of Mr. Gishard for she comes back as a poltergeist to torment the living.

In the story's second section, the narrator's mother is introduced as one of the characters who can use magic. In fact, the mother is identified as a "changer," one who can change anything. She not only changes wet sheets into dry ones, but she also changes herself. The girl, too, changes in the night. But instead of taking on magical powers, she regresses to an earlier stage of development. She devolves into an infantile state in which she has no power to control herself or those who surround her.

Throughout the story, the world of night is unstable and disorienting. It is contrasted with a daylight reality that is relatively knowable, for on the other side of darkness magic does not rule the day. However, in the third section the night is also presented as offering a comfortable side. Here the girl meets her father, whom she describes as a "very nice and very kind . . . night-soil man" (9). He brings her warmth and happiness, and he even promises to take her to the circus (10).

The fourth section of the story returns to a vision of the night as threatening. Here even the natural world is threatened, as the vexed "flowers close up and thicken" (10). The predictable then becomes unpredictable and magic is used to perpetuate violence: someone sprinkles a "colorless powder outside a closed door so that someone else's child will be stillborn" (11).

The story concludes with the girl's fairytale vision of a happy ending. She conjures up an image of comfort and security by fantasizing about how she would like to unite with another woman (a loving and maternal figure) and live with her in domestic bliss. In this fantasy, the woman becomes the girl's protector, and she offers the child a space whereby she can return to the warmth and comfort of the woman's womb. It is through this retreat, this devolution, that the girl believes she can be "completely happy" (12).

"At Last"

The third story in the collection, "At Last," is divided into two sections: "The House" and "The Yard." By separating the story into these two sections, Kincaid moves the narrative from the internal, domesticated area of the house to the external, bordered landscape of the garden. The first section focuses on the relationship between a mother and a daughter, and the text begins when the daughter interrogates her mother about her early childhood, about how things were when she was an infant. The daughter longs to remember this time; in fact, she becomes almost obsessed with her prememory and the developmental relationship between her mother and herself. The daughter, who narrates much of the story, wants to hold onto her past. She also expresses a desire to remain in her childhood state, to reject growth and maturity in favor of innocence and dependence. This desire is caught up in a fantasy wherein the protagonist sees herself as remaining intimately tied to her mother, for she wants to retain the strong bond that is slowly weakening with time and age.

In much of the story, the voices of mother and daughter are difficult to distinguish from each other. Their voices often merge, suggesting that their lives are intimately intertwined. However, such a merger also anticipates an inevitable rupture, for the development of the daughter's individuality will eventually lead to a disintegration of the union. At the same time, though, the domestic life of the house triggers the daughter's desire to piece together the history of her prememory. "I lived in this house with you," the daughter says, "the wood shingles, unpainted, weather-beaten, fraying; the piano, a piece of furniture now, collecting dust; the bed in which all the children are born" (13). The domestic space and the list of objects in the house become an attempt at jogging her lost memories as she tries to figure out the conditions of her early life. But the voice can also be read as an appeal, for the girl wants her mother to confirm that this was the house where she was born and the place where their relationship began. Here the bed is significant. For it is the place where her mother gave birth to her, marking the moment of separation between mother and daughter as well as the point of origin for the relationship that will come to define their lives. But the bed is also the place where the protagonist's siblings are born, and these births are also responsible for ruptures in the mother-daughter union.

The daughter, though, soon discovers that she cannot uncover the past. Her questions only lead to more questions. "What are you now?" she asks, "A young woman. But what are you really?" (13). One query leads to another and the daughter is unable to envision a reliable image of the past. She cannot rely on her mother's answers, which often remain elusive and vague. For example, when the daughter asks the crucial question, "So I was loved?" her mother responds with a non sequitur: "Yes. You wore your clothes wrapped tight around your body, keeping your warmth to yourself. What greed!" (16). And throughout the story, when the daughter repeatedly asks questions about "the light," the mother remains silent. The question is asked four times ("What was that light?"; "Was that the light again?") and each time the mother refuses to respond. The daughter is, like the reader, left to speculate about what the light really is. The light could represent the elusiveness of enlightenment. Her desire to know—her need to shed light on the past—is suggested in the repetition of this flickering, yet momentary, flash of light. The illumination, though, is fleeting. In the end she does not know if she has seen the light, and she will never know the past because her attempt to regain history by remembering its lost details will always fail.

In the conclusion of the story, the narrative moves outside. Here nature is presented as being more powerful than humanity. People can influence nature for a short period (a person has planted bluebells for the child's garden), but human intervention is not lasting. Eventually the work of the gardener will be undone, for the cycle of life demands that the bluebells will, in the autumn, whither and fall to the ground. Change and death are thus depicted as part of the natural rhythms and flows of nature. But recognizing this cycle does not necessarily offer the protagonist a compelling answer to the questions she poses. "What is anything after it is dead and gone?" she asks (19). Her sense of loss cannot be overcome by linking her experience to the inevitable cycle of life and death. She still seeks answers and looks for the light.

"Wingless"

In "Wingless," the young girl at the center of the story makes the transition from the domestic environment to the public realm of the school and socialization. This is the first major separation of the mother from the child. Thus the story explores the first step toward the individuality of the child. The institutional space of the school forces the daughter out of the home and offers her a place to develop beyond the view of her mother's gaze. This stage of development is represented in both positive and negative ways. On the one hand, it is described as a time of "discovery" and endless possibilities (24). The change is exciting and dramatic for the girl; she feels a sense of freedom now that she has left the suffocating embrace of her mother (27). On the other hand, the girl is overwhelmed by fear of what she sees as her own shortcomings. Her process of self-discovery, then, includes a complex network of emotions, moving from liberation and terror to excitement and alienation.

As the title suggests, the girl of the story is still "wingless." And yet the protagonist realizes that her wings are beginning to grow. She has reached the point at which she must acquire the physical, emotional, and psychological traits that will enable her to leave the nest. Part of this psychic development is being sensitive to the world outside the home; she must learn the social codes and cultural practices of the public realm. "I shall try to see clearly," she says, "I shall try to tell differences" (22). As a result, she begins to note differences in the objects around her (such as the colors of fine cloth). But these observations soon give way to the recognition of larger differences: she begins to see distinctions between herself and her mother, and she starts to realize that people are different—some children are worthy of her friendship and others are not.

Her catalog of differences then transforms into a lack of self-confidence. "My charm is limited," she says, "I haven't learned to smile yet. . . . I am so unhappy, my face is so wet" (23). The journey to find herself and the path of self-discovery is sometimes painful and difficult. She must learn to accept herself and to avoid self-hate. Yet still further difficulties arise out of her attempts to separate herself from her mother, for she desires the break but also fears it. What will she become when the separation is complete? How will she find her way in the world? Who will love her in the future? These questions echo throughout her mind and force her to turn away from the "brink of great discovery" (24). The protagonist, then, retreats into the comforting wings of her mother. But as in "Girl," the mother's protective wings suddenly transform into aggressive weapons. The mother begins to mock her daughter for the very fears and anxieties that she has instilled in the child.

"Wingless" concludes like the previous story: it ends with a meditation on the natural world. The powerful image of the Caribbean Sea—"so smooth [but with] a great and swift undercurrent"—mesmerizes the girl and even follows her home, "snapping at [her] heels" (25–26). Here the all-encompassing power of nature is presented as an alternative to the power of her mother, for the maternal power has no dominion over the forces of the natural world. In nature life moves (slowly or suddenly) into death: the quick lizard and the slow ant will eventually grow still. This stillness—this death—is, by the end of the story, the only answer offered to the questions that the girl has posed. She seeks the liberation of a great discovery, but her search only leads her to a recognition that mortality is universal, and she thus comes face to face with her own future "stillness."

"Holidays"

"Holidays" is one of the few short stories by Kincaid that is not set in the Caribbean. Here the protagonist has left the home and traveled to a new place (which seems to be the United States) where she is both free and disoriented. The voice of the first-person narrator has escaped from the small place of her home, but this escape has brought with it a sense of aimlessness and wandering. Beginning at a holiday house in the mountains, the main character gazes about the yard, making note of the flies and butterflies. A bee then appears and this reminds her of her mother: "If you sit with your hands on your head," she thinks, "you will kill your mother" (31). In this stream of consciousness style, the bee, with its capacity to sting, leads the character to consider the love-hate relationship that she has with her mother. Her fantasy of murdering her mother, however innocent the superstition might be, then prompts feelings of guilt and shame.

As one thought leads to another, the protagonist considers writing a letter. But whom will she write to? "Dear So and So," she thinks, and then she drops the idea and returns to a consideration of her surroundings. At the end of the first section, she is tired of her dull "holiday" and she dreams of yet another escape: "I will have a dream," she thinks, "a dream in which I am not sitting on the porch facing the mountains" (32).

The emptiness of holidays (and tourism in general) is further explored in the next section when a variety of unidentified tourists speak superficially about their travel arrangements and itineraries. They tell of having the perfect luggage and driving on scenic roads in the country. They speak of gazing into a sunset, which they judge to be far "too orange" (33). Likewise, the pebbles are said to be "not pebbly enough," but the house they pass on the road does have some "interesting angles" (32). This part of the story anticipates *A Small Place*, which is Kincaid's in-depth critique of Western tourism, consumption, and exploitation. The tourists are depicted as only thinking about their own entertainment; they do not always respect the natural world or the native inhabitants of the places they have come to visit.

Much can go wrong on a holiday, and the protagonist composes a list of the bad things that might happen to her during her trip. She might get hurt playing with a ball; the dog might get sprayed by a skunk; she might get stung by an insect. More serious, though, is having a case of sunstroke, and the speaker does fall victim to this condition. Here, as in Kincaid's other stories, the reader witnesses the power of the light. The sun might be attractive and even beautiful, but it is also potentially dangerous. Its strength can burn one's skin and result in illness. By extension, the power of the sun is also, symbolically speaking, linked to the power of enlightenment. For enlightenment can bring understanding, but it can also result in pain and suffering.

The protagonist then moves from thinking about light to a consideration of seeing. She witnesses a blind man, and she constructs a narrative wherein the man has been blinded by love. She states that the man became blind after he discovered his wife to be unfaithful, for in a furious rage he murdered her and blinded himself in a failed attempt to commit suicide. Here love is depicted as a destructive force: the man kills the woman he loves and then robs himself of light and vision. He has become a kind of zombie—one of the walking dead—who does not speak as he wanders alone on the empty streets.

The old man sparks the protagonist's memory of her blinding and murderous love for her mother. He thus becomes a source of fear and anxiety for her, and she tries to escape from him by returning to the dullness of her holiday. The final part of the story is made up of a series of impressions about her journey: the water, the postcards, the laughter. This is a fragmented and disjointed conclusion. And the fragmentation seems to suggest that the protagonist is attempting to avoid serious thoughts by focusing on trivial matters. In the end, though, her disconnected thoughts only lead in circles, never taking her forward on her journey through life.

"The Letter from Home"

"The Letter from Home" is, like "Girl," approximately three pages in length and made up of one long sentence. Once again the voice is powerful and dominating, but this time the reader is not sure who is speaking. The text seems to combine the voices of mother and daughter, as the narrator moves from a commentary on domestic life to mythical and religious questions to expressions of pain and anger. As the title suggests, the text is constructed around a series of epistles from home. Indeed in the story the daughter has left home, and the letters are meant to inform her of what has been happening at home since her departure. But the letters inevitably spark memories and emotions that the daughter is trying to forget. Home is a place from which she might try to free herself, but the letters will always follow her, and these texts will not allow her to forget what she is trying to leave behind. Home will always catch up with her.

The story begins with a list of the everyday work that needs to be done around the house. "I milked the cows, I churned the butter, I stored the cheese, I baked the bread, I brewed the tea" (37). The tasks carried out in this domestic space are then described as threatening: "The pot boiled, the gas hissed through the stove, the tree branches heavy with snow crashed against the roof, my heart beat loudly *thud! thud!,* tiny beads of water gathered on my nose . . . lips trembled, tears have flowed, cheeks have puffed, stomachs have twisted with pain" (37). This section of the letter is not an innocent account of news from home, nor is it an expression of love. Instead it chronicles the grief and pain of the domestic scene, and it transmits the sadness and loss of those who are left behind.

This is one of the most surreal stories in the collection. One image transforms into another, just as one feeling sparks other emotions. For instance, the domestic scene at the beginning soon melts into a consideration of spiritual and religious matters: "Is the Heaven to be above? Is the Hell below? Does the Lamb lie meek? Does the Lion roar?" (38). The grounded landscape of everyday life leads to an abstract consideration of metaphysical issues. What life lies beyond this one? Where does this life lead? What is the relation between this world and another realm? These questions are invoked but never answered. But they do lead to images that provoke visions of the relationship between history and home. The speaker then focuses on a "peninsula" where some "ancient ships are still anchored" (38). Perhaps these are the ships of the middle passage—ships that transported slaves from their home on another continent to a small foreign island in the Caribbean. The ancient ships, then, speak to the protagonist's own journey from home, but they also raise much larger questions about one's homeland. Where is home? Is it where the protagonist is born? Or is it a place (perhaps an imagined place) that goes back to a time before slavery and the displacement of Africans?

This image is then related to the mother's condemnation of her daughter's departure. Leaving home, the mother suggests, perpetuates loss and can result in tragic consequences. From this perspective the daughter's life abroad does not only disrupt the family, but it also disturbs the natural flow of history. For the mother's voice suggests that the daughter belongs at home—she should live in her "motherland"—and she should return to the place where she was born.

"What I Have Been Doing Lately"

In this story Kincaid returns to the voice of a young girl. This narrative is particularly surreal and dreamlike, for the protagonist speaks in a circular fashion of leaving home and returning. As a result, the story reflects upon the gains and losses of growing up. And the excitement of entering the world is mixed with the desire to return home and erase the journey beyond the domestic realm of innocence and maternal security. But once the girl has left the house, she will never be able to go back to what existed before.

The story recounts two different versions of similar events. The first version begins with the girl lying in bed when she hears the doorbell ring. She goes to answer the door, but nobody is there. She then goes outside, leaving the house behind her, and enters an atmosphere filled with either drizzle or dust that "tasted like government school ink" (40). This surreal image connects the protagonist's exiting of the house with the child's first separation from the home as she begins her daily routine of going to school. However, this story is not about school; it is about exploring the world. Soon after she begins her exploration, the girl encounters a body of water that blocks her path. But she does not let this stop her; she pushes on by building a boat to row across the water. This task consumes much time, but eventually she succeeds, and her hard work is rewarded when the boat carries her to the other side.

A person then appears in the distance. As the figure comes toward her, the girl believes it to be her mother. But she is mistaken. The girl does not recognize the woman, but the woman clearly knows the girl. "It's you," the strange woman says to the girl, "Just look at that. It's you. And just what have you been doing lately?" (43). The girl considers the question before giving the stranger an answer. Should she tell the truth? Which of the many recent events in her life should she reveal? Should she confess her inner thoughts? Perhaps not.

The girl chooses to tell the same story that she has just been narrating to the reader. At first the girl's retelling of the narrative is identical to what she has already stated. As the tale continues, though, the reader begins to see shifts in the language and changes in the action. For instance, she changes her account of the sky, and her second description of the monkey is changed from a passive meeting to a violent confrontation. She throws four stones at the monkey, and he retaliates by catching the fourth stone and throwing it back, wounding her on the forehead. Thus the second account of the events is much more challenging and aggressive than the first. She no longer gazes at the world, overwhelmed by its force. Instead she interacts with the outside world, grappling with antagonists and exerting her power.

The two accounts differ in significant ways. In the first telling the girl falls into a deep hole—a dark abyss—but she escapes from it without any injuries. In the second version her journey is much more difficult. She finds herself exhausted and unable to locate a comforting and homely place. "If only just around the bend," she thinks, "I would see my house and inside my house I would find a bed . . . and I would find my mother or anyone else that I loved making me custard" (45). But she cannot find her home. The new world is, in the end, harsh and tiring, and she comes to the realization that she can never go home again. All she can do is repeat the story from the beginning, so she concludes the narrative where she starts, "lying in bed, just before the doorbell rang" (45).

"Blackness"

"Blackness" is one of the most challenging stories in the book. This is because Kincaid uses the image of blackness to convey conflicting ideas: blackness is presented as an image of annihilation and erasure, but it is also depicted as an image of renewal and rebirth. As a result, the story is ambiguous, elusive, and fragmented. Indeed, throughout the narrative, blackness confounds oppositional thinking by breaking down binaries and bringing opposites together. Blackness is the night that transforms day into darkness, but it is also the color of a racial identity, a color that "flows through . . . veins" (46).

Kincaid uses "blackness" to disturb the order and logic of Western rationalism. In this story things are not separated into clear-cut categories or compartments, for the order of Enlightenment rationalism has been overshadowed by darkness. This reordering of experience is a challenge to Western hierarchies that have relegated blackness to a position of inferiority. After all, European languages have always defined blackness as something to fear, as something to overcome, and as something to dominate. In racial terms, blackness has been placed in direct opposition to whiteness, and, as such, black bodies have been relegated to the margins through a history of exploitation, bondage, and slavery. In Kincaid's text, though, blackness is not only responsible for silence, erasure, and annihilation; it also provides a deeply complex vision of selfhood and identity formation. She thus develops a paradox in which the loss of the self comes to define the self.

For instance, the second section of "Blackness" describes an invading army. These "bands of men" walk aimlessly with "their guns and cannons," fighting at random until "they grew tied of it" (49). The soldiers are responsible for creating darkness across the land, for they "blot . . . out the daylight" and cause "night to [fall] immediately and permanently" (49). The speaker of the story describes the blackness that surrounds her: she can no longer see the flowers or the animals in the pasture. Here blackness is connected to cruelty, oppression, and violence. And the brutal army is depicted as going against nature, while at the same time conveying the historical reality of the invasion of the Caribbean by European armies. This "black" history is a source of depression for the speaker, as the soldiers are said to "march through [her] house," destroying everything in their path (49). This image not only captures the personal trauma of the protagonist, but it also speaks to the traumas of those who have been conquered by European settlers. The protagonist's house can be read as symbolic of the Caribbean island itself—an island upon which the white army has marched and spread destruction.

The next section consists of a mother's description of her daughter. This part envisions a loving and nurturing mother-daughter relationship that is devoid of the destructive elements that appear in some of the other stories. Here maternal love is depicted as a positive source of energy that can help to engender the child's identity and allow the daughter's sense of self to grow. Throughout this section, the mother seems to recognize the importance of her role as a nurturer: she reports on her daughter's growth and she is proud of her child's development. In the face of "blackness" and the negation of self, there is a sense of hope that the loving mother can offer the tools and space needed for the child's development, her individuation.

The concluding section moves from "blackness" to silence. In fact, the protagonist is said to "move toward" a silent voice that embraces her so that "even in memory the blackness is erased"

(52). This is important, for the blackness in the first section was responsible for erasing the identity of the main character. Here, though, blackness itself is subject to erasure and completely forgotten. The silence that follows the blackness is, the narrative suggests, the next stage in the process of the character's development. The protagonist has moved out of the blackness of the abyss to a silent world where, in order to develop further, she must begin to find her own voice. By the end of the story, the narrator is "at peace" (52). She might be engulfed in silence, but she recognizes that she is moving in the right direction.

"My Mother"

"My Mother" begins with the voice of a daughter wishing that her mother were dead. But the articulation of this wish is immediately followed by remorse, and the daughter drenches the earth with a riverlike flood of tears. She begs her mother's forgiveness. And the mother responds with a suffocating embrace that almost robs the girl of life. Here Kincaid once again explores the complexities of a love-hate relationship between a mother and a daughter. In this introductory scene, the murderous love is first articulated and put into language to devastating effect: its utterance results in a profound separation between the two characters and leaves a permanent gulf that can never be bridged. If "What I Have Been Doing Lately" suggests that the girl can never go home again, "My Mother" implies that words, once uttered, can never be taken back.

The mother of the story does not know why this breach has developed between them. She thinks that perhaps it is the result of an evil spell, so she turns to the magic of an obeah ceremony to address the problem. Shutting herself and her daughter in a room, the mother darkens the space by blocking the entrance.

She then lights candles in order to cast shadows and watches the shadows to see if they can uncover the source of the spell. The shadows "make a place between themselves, as if they were making room for someone else," but the space continues to remain empty and the mother is unable to read the signs that would solve the mystery of their estrangement.

Although the obeah ceremony does not reveal the author of the spell, the mother continues to use magic in the third section of the story. Here she transforms from a woman into a serpent-like creature with scales and flattened eyes on the top of her head. The eyes are described as particularly threatening for they spin and blaze wildly. The metamorphosis increases the mother's power over her daughter, and she commands the child to undergo a similar transformation. The girl obeys her mother, and both figures begin to move snakelike on the floor, traveling on their white underbellies with their "tongue[s] darting and flickering in the hot air" (55). The daughter seems to be under the spell of the mother, but by mimicking her parent, the child also demonstrates her own potential to become powerful and threatening. She, like her mother, can also transform herself into a venomous creature.

The development of the daughter's power continues in the next section. Here the girl is growing into a young woman, and although the mother still exerts power over her, the daughter sees herself getting bigger and bigger. Indeed the mother has taught the daughter to empower herself through manipulation, and the daughter/pupil now realizes that she can use this power against her mother/teacher. There is still a bond connecting the two characters, a bond that will always reinstate a hierarchy whereby the mother can disempower her daughter by reducing her to the level of the child.

As the daughter gets larger and larger, so, too, does her mother. But in section five, they both enter a cold and dark cave. The daughter remains there for years. Her eyes adapt to the lack of light, and she finds a "special coat" to keep herself warm. Instead of supporting her child, the mother verbally abuses the daughter, attacking her for being unable to adapt to a place "not suited to [her] nature" (57). But the daughter strikes back. She tries to trap her mother by building a beautiful house over a deep hole and inviting her mother inside; she dreams that her mother will enter the house and then fall "with a thud" to the bottom of the hole (58). She wants to rob her mother of her maternal powers by forcing her to live in the pit. In the end, though, the mother cannot be captured. She is too clever and strong for that, and when she enters the mock house, she is able to walk on the air, resisting the gulf of the cavernous abyss.

By the end of the story, the daughter has come to terms with her mother's superior powers. She will never be able to beat her mother on her own ground. As a result, the daughter's only choice is to leave, so she sets off on a voyage across the sea. On the other side of the ocean, the girl meets another woman (another mother), who embraces her and takes her home. This new mother is juxtaposed to the mother of the earlier sections. Where the old mother was mocking, manipulative, and threatening, the new one is kind, nurturing, and loving. The girl then develops a marriagelike bond with the woman: "As we talked," the girl says, "our voices became one voice, and we were in complete union in every other way" (59). The story has a happy ending: the girl has given up fighting with her mother and formed a harmonious union with another woman. The conclusion depicts the girl believing that she has finally found a "home" and that she will have a bright future.

"At the Bottom of the River"

This last story of the collection depicts the girl's final development to maturity. Here the voice of the mother is no longer dominant. Rather the girl has become the woman; she has gained her own voice and developed a strong sense of self. At this stage of her life, she has become part of the world, and she is happy with her newfound identity, for even her own name now "fill[s] up" her mouth" (82). But her gain is also accompanied by a sense of loss. Her new life is accompanied by a knowledge of her own mortality; she now knows that death will eventually catch up with her, and her maturity goes hand-in-hand with a recognition that she will, like everything else, grow old and die.

Throughout this short story cycle, Kincaid has played with the metaphor of the "journey of life." And in this final story, the journey metaphor is transformed into the image of the river. Life flows like the force and energy of a stream—they both twist, turn, and eventually come to rest in the calm pool. Life corresponds to the rush of the water, whereas death is tied to the collected water in the pool and the things at the bottom of the river.

The narrator then examines the ebbs and flows of two types of men. The first is the life of the European male colonizer. He cannot recognize the beauty of the world, and he is dead to the energy and potential that surrounds him. He cannot comprehend anything beyond his own frame of reference, nor can he understand those whom he disempowers. He is, in short, empty and defined by his nothingness. The second man is a character who resembles Kincaid's stepfather—the carpenter of *Annie John* and the father she describes in her *New Yorker* articles. This man is not alienated from the world around him; he thrives on the beauty and energy of the river. However, he is a colonized subject, and as such his life is limited by his marginal position and disempowerment. He too is "nothing," and his life is ruled by a condition of emptiness.

The story then returns to the contemplation of death articulated in the first section. The speaker becomes overwhelmed by a sense of depression at the inevitability of death. "Death is the past," she says, "Dead shall the future be" (69). Death might be natural, but it brings on grief, loss, and mourning. As a result, she laments the lost innocence of her childhood—a time when she was not aware of the power of death. But this lament is short lived, and the speaker soon returns to the water of life, celebrating its power and force.

It is in the water that the woman can find herself. As she gazes into the liquid, she sees a house, a homely place where a kind and welcoming woman lives. The woman encourages the speaker to see in new ways and to accept the world around her. As her eyes begin to focus more clearly, the speaker recognizes that the woman in the water is really herself. For the first time, she has a clear view of herself, as if she is "looking through a pane of glass" and seeing every delightful detail of her newfound identity (79). By accepting the world as it is, the narrative suggests, one can find one's self and see one's surroundings in the proper light.

Now that the woman has found herself she can enter the water. The image of the water thus transforms into a source of life and cleansing. She "dips" into the water "again and again, over and over," and the bathing connects her to nature as well as to the forces and energies of the universe (80). It is through this cleansing and connectedness that she comes to see "a reflecting light," a "light that can never be destroyed" (80). By literally "seeing the light," the protagonist witnesses something that will not die. For "the light" cannot be destroyed and, as a result, offers her a source of hope beyond the grief of inevitable loss and mourning. Whatever this light is—and its meaning remains unclear—the woman embraces it as a basis of beauty in the world.

At the Bottom of the River shows the development of a protagonist from girlhood to maturity. The stories move from the passive child of "Girl" through the girl's assertion of independence in "What I Have Been Doing Lately" to the girl leaving home in "My Mother" to the girl becoming the woman in "At the Bottom of the River." Throughout these stories, Kincaid offers the reader intimate first-person voices, and she treats her subjects with depth and complexity. The stories can also be read as early explorations of the central themes that Kincaid will develop in all of her major works.

CHAPTER 3

Early Novels
Annie John and *Lucy*

Annie John

In many respects, Kincaid's first novel, *Annie John* (1985), expands upon the themes, motifs, images, and ideas explored in *At the Bottom of the River*. Life and death, loss and mourning, mother and daughter, childhood and maturity—all of these subjects appear and reappear throughout Kincaid's early writing. Moreover, like *At the Bottom of the River*, *Annie John* began as a series of stories and sketches for the *New Yorker*. After appearing in the magazine, the individual pieces were compiled and edited into the novel, which was published to wide critical acclaim in 1985. The initial reviews were extremely positive, with critics calling it "touching and familiar" and "emotionally powerful."[1] More recent critical evaluations of *Annie John* have also praised the book. For instance, writing in 2003, Amy Levin applauded Kincaid's depictions of female characters who are able to resist racism, sexism, and colonial subjugation by creating a personal space in which African traditions and European culture are intertwined. And in 2004 Babacar M'Baye wrote that the power of *Annie John* lies in Kincaid's ability to represent women who "transform themselves and resist male dominance," highlighting the "spiritual power and agency of black women."[2]

Annie John is Kincaid's first full-length examination of a girl growing up in Antigua, a subject she will return to in some of her later works. The text, which follows Annie's growth, can be read as a bildungsroman. It is, among other things, a coming-of-age novel about the discovery of the self that recounts the process of individual development and learning about the world. As a result, it is appropriate that *Annie John* is narrated in retrospect by Annie herself: the first chapter begins "during the year I was ten," and the last chapter relates "the last day I spent in Antigua," six years later.[3] Kincaid thus adheres to the bildungsroman genre by mapping out Annie's physical and spiritual growth alongside her loss of innocence and her acquisition of maturity. Indeed, throughout the novel, Annie's first-person narration captures her adolescent struggles as she is faced with traditional gender roles, deals with her troubled relationship to her mother, develops a growing awareness of imperialism, and forms friendships with her peers. By the end of the novel, Annie has passed through the stages of schooling, puberty, adolescence, and she has emerged as a young adult. It is then that she decides to leave the small island of her youth.

And yet it must be noted that Kincaid adds her own ingredients to the white, European tradition of the bildungsroman. (This genre is often associated with male writers such as Charles Dickens, James Joyce, and Mark Twain.) In *Annie John,* Kincaid explores unique subject matters and content that distinguish her text from the male, European or American content of the genre. Kincaid's treatment of Caribbean life, mother-daughter relations, sexual development, and the critique of European imperialism can be read as a reworking of the genre. Annie, in other words, grows up in a culturally specific milieu that has a profound impact on the development of her individuality. The small community on this Caribbean island effects Annie's subject formation, and it is this cultural specificity that distinguishes Kincaid's novel from the traditional bildungsroman. In the end,

Annie's maturity is not marked by her integration into the community. Rather her maturity goes hand-in-hand with her rejection of Antigua through emigration.

Annie John is also a text that incorporates autobiographical material. In an interview in 1990, Kincaid admitted to the personal content of her first novel: "The feelings in it [*Annie John*] are autobiographical, yes. I didn't want to say it was autobiographical because I felt that would be somehow admitting something about myself, but it is and so that's that."[4] Certainly the text expresses Annie's powerful emotions, her conflicting feelings, as well as her complex responses to her early experiences. And perhaps it is the personal nature of those feelings that inspired Kincaid to write the novel in such a direct and accessible style. Literary critics such as Diane Simmons have noted that *Annie John* is written in a fluid and coherent style; it thus departs from the fragmentation and surrealism that was present in *At the Bottom of the River*.[5] But the text's linear structure does not make *Annie John* a simple novel. For what lies behind the descriptions of cooking and schooling, the pleasures of early friendship and reading books, are images of death and loss, depression and mourning, history and colonization. As in "At the Bottom of the River," the protagonist's maturity brings with it a recognition of universal mortality through the loss of innocence and the subsequent death of the child within.

The subject of death is introduced in the first sentence of the novel: "During the year I was ten," Annie John states, "I thought only people I did not know died" (3). In fact, this retrospective meditation on death is followed by a description of the cemetery that lies beside the family's temporary home. The ten-year-old Annie watches from her yard as "sticklike figures, some dressed in black," bury the dead in the distance (4). When Annie returns home and describes this scene to her mother, she is told that the "stick figures" are probably burying a child, because children are buried in the morning. This is the moment that Annie learns that children can die, and soon after this she hears about the death of Nalda, a young girl who dies in the arms of Annie's mother. Nalda's death, then, shatters Annie's naive notions of life and mortality. She is now faced with the fact that all things (even children) die. This chain of events moves fluidly from the child seeing the cemetery, where death is off in the distance, to the closeness of Nalda's death and the rupture of her childhood illusion. Annie's notion of death is destroyed when Nalda dies, and this event leads her one step closer to realizing her own mortality. This opening scene presents the reader with one of the most important themes of the book: a child's innocence will gradually recede into the past, no matter how hard he or she tries to hold onto it.

Annie then becomes haunted by death. "I was afraid of death," she admits, "as was everyone I knew" (4). Indeed, for the ten-year-old Annie, the dead "might show up again" at anytime; they might "follow you home" and then wait for you so that they could "follow you wherever you went" (4). Throughout the text, life is seen to be a struggle to avoid death, particularly the death of childhood and the death of the spirit. And Annie's constant return to this subject borders on an obsession. But this is not surprising when the reader considers that death is seen to go hand-in-hand with maturity. For her, development is associated with the process of confronting the deaths of people around her, and as her knowledge of mortality touches closer to home, Annie begins to associate death with her mother. Her mother has given her children life, but she is also, from Annie's perspective, often present when people die. In fact, when Annie hears that Nalda has died in her mother's hands, she begins to see her mother as a carrier of death. "I then began to look at my mother's hands differently," Annie says, "They had stroked the dead girl's forehead; they had bathed and dressed her and laid her in the coffin. . . . I could not bear to have my mother caress me or touch my food or help me with my bath" (6). In Annie's mind, her mother's hands are no longer nurturing or life affirming; they are now associated with the death of Nalda and with death itself. Annie then asks herself if her mother will kill her too, but the question remains unanswered. As a precaution, Annie begins silently to distance herself from her mother, and the process of association that links her mother to death begins to foreshadow Annie's later perception of her mother as someone who stifles and suffocates her.

Later in the novel, the mother's hand is again equated with death. Here Annie has returned home from Sunday school earlier than expected, and she secretly sees her parents in bed together. Her mother's hand caresses her father's back as she kisses his ears, his mouth, and his face. "But her hand," Annie states, "was white and bony, as if it had long been dead. . . . It seemed not to be her hand, and yet it could only be her hand, so well did I know it. . . . I looked at it as if I would never see anything else in my life again" (30–31). For Annie, this is a powerful moment of betrayal. She witnesses her mother's affection being given to someone else, and she begins to see her mother as false, hypocritical, and lifeless. The hand that caresses her father—a hand that is, for Annie, only meant to caress and comfort her—is now cold, white, and dead. Annie's response moves from feeling betrayed to emotions of jealousy and anger, inspiring her to reject her mother. "I could never let those hands touch me again," she says, "I was sure I could never let her kiss me again. All that was finished" (32). This is yet another moment of lost innocence. Annie's strong reaction derives from jealousy, but her intense feelings also arise because she is, for the first time, seeing her mother as a sexual subject. In this scene, Annie witnesses another side of her mother's identity: she is not just the loving, maternal figure Annie has come to adore; she is also a wife and lover to Annie's father. This moment of recognition forces Annie to glimpse what she is expected to become. Eventually she will be forced to leave the comfort of her mother's home (as well as the playful world of her girlfriends) and enter a male-dominated society where she will be expected to develop a bond with a man.

Death, then, is related to motherly love. And throughout the text, death is a kind of betrayal that is associated with the mother abandoning her child. The breach that will develop between Annie and her mother is present as early as the first two chapters. And Annie seems to glimpse a future that holds a deterioration of the mother-daughter relationship and the death of her childhood. In fact, Annie's obsession with death causes an early distancing from her mother. This occurs when Annie begins to attend the funerals of anonymous people without her mother's permission. (Annie likes to visit the funeral parlor where the dead are laid out for viewing.) On one occasion, when Annie goes to the funeral of a hunchback girl, she returns home late and has forgotten to buy the fish, as her mother had instructed. Instead of confessing to her transgression, Annie decides to lie, telling her mother that Mr. Earl, the fisherman, had not gone to sea that day. But her mother catches her in the lie and punishes her for it. Annie is forced to eat dinner outside, away from the family, and her mother sends her to bed without a good night kiss. Annie's lie, as well as the punishment that follows, is presented as yet another event that contributes to the breakdown of the mother-daughter relationship.

Annie's father is also connected to death. After all, he is a carpenter who builds, among other things, coffins. At the beginning of the story, for instance, he makes the coffin for Nalda, and later in the text Annie hears that he built a casket for his own grandmother. Indeed, in the second chapter, Annie's father tells her about how he was raised by his grandmother and that she loved and cared for him until she died when he was eighteen. He recounts how he slept in his grandmother's bed, and that one morning he overslept because she did not wake him up. When he awoke, she was lying dead beside him; she had died in her sleep sometime during the night. Although her father was "overwhelmed with grief," he tells Annie, he still "built her coffin and made sure she had a nice funeral" (23). When her father finishes the story, Annie begins to weep. The loss of the maternal figure and the sense of her father being alone in the world are too much for her to bear. "I loved him so," she says of her father at that moment, "and wished that I had a mother to give him, for, no matter how much my own mother loved him, it could never be the same" (24). Here Annie expresses her belief that a mother's love is invaluable and that maternal love, once lost, can never be replaced. But in the scene Annie's sympathy soon turns to empathy. She moves from feeling sorry for her father to recognizing that she too will one day suffer from the same loss. It is only when Annie's mother returns and assures her child that she will never "sail off" or "die" or "leave [Annie] all alone in the world" that Annie stops weeping (24).

The onset of puberty signals the imminent death of Annie's powerful bond to her mother. As Annie's body begins to change, her mother forces her to wear new clothes. Up to this point the mother and daughter have always worn dresses from the same material. But as Annie reaches puberty, her mother forces her to wear clothes made from a different material: "You just cannot go around the rest of your life looking like a little me," she tells Annie (26). The symbolism here is striking: mother and daughter are no longer cut from the same cloth. Annie's new clothing marks her as being different from her mother (forging yet another division between them), but the new clothes also imply that Annie must develop her own sense of self that is distinct and unique. From the mother's perspective, she is doing what is best for her daughter; she is helping Annie become an independent young woman. From Annie's perspective, though, the new clothes are yet another betrayal, and she responds by "feeling bitterness and hatred" toward her mother (26).

Annie comes to see her growth as responsible for her mother's changing attitudes. As a result, she dreams about acquiring a "set of clamps" that she can screw on at night in order to stunt her growth (27). She even identifies her maturation—what her mother calls "becoming a young lady"—as that which destroys the "perfect harmony" that she has previously experienced with her mother (27). But this "young-lady business" cannot be stopped, and her mother continues to "turn away" from her (28). Annie then tries to replace her mother's love by "falling in love" with Gwen, a young girl who attends the same school. In fact, by the end of her first day of classes Annie says, "Gwen and I were in love, and so we walked home arm in arm together" (33). Annie's love for Gwen comes to stand in for the "perfect harmony" that she has had with her mother. But this love will also die. On the day that Annie begins to menstruate, Annie, Gwen, and her other girlfriends congregate at the graveyard to discuss Annie's development. The graveyard is of course a significant setting in that it once again signals death: the death of Annie's girlhood and the loss of her harmonious relationship with Gwen. For as the girls leave the graveyard and return to class, Annie feels "as if she is going to a funeral" (53). "Gwen and I," she narrates, "vowed to love each other always, but the words had a hollow ring, and when we looked at each other we couldn't sustain the gaze" (53). Their love is not, as Annie desires, eternal. Rather it is yet another stage in Annie's personal development.

Annie's love then shifts from Gwen to the Red Girl. Here Annie is not only trying to replace her mother's love, but she is also rebelling against her mother. The Red Girl is not someone whom Annie's mother would call "ladylike": she does not wash regularly, her clothes are usually dirty, she climbs trees, and she loves to play marbles with boys. Annie considers the Red Girl "a beautiful thing," an "angel," whom she cannot help but love (57). Her relationship with the Red Girl begins to grow, and they meet each day at the abandoned lighthouse. Annie must keep this union a secret from her mother, for whereas Gwen "met with [her] mother's complete approval," the Red Girl is "one of those girls who lik[ed] to play marbles" —the type of girl Annie's mother hates (61). Annie relishes this secret as well as the knowledge of her mother's disapproval. In fact, the Red Girl offers an alternative to the strict "ladylike" gender codes that are enforced by Annie's mother, for the Red Girl resists the constraints and expectations attached to the "young-lady business" so despised by Annie, but which are so valued by her mother. From Annie's perspective, the Red Girl crosses gender boundaries and is thus "better than any boy" (56). This certainly accounts for Annie's deep admiration, affection, and devotion for her new friend.

Annie's rebellious behavior further establishes difference from her mother, constituting an assertion of her individuality. However, Annie also sees the secretive nature of the relationship as an act of "betraying" her mother; she believes that her mother has betrayed her, and now she seeks her revenge (59). Annie's betrayal leads to a series of lies, manipulations, and deceptions that include everything from making up elaborate stories to stealing money to hiding marbles under the house. All of this comes to a climax when her mother discovers that Annie has been playing marbles and hiding her winnings. This is described as a devastating moment for Annie ("everything was over," she thinks) not just because she has angered her mother but because her mother will put a stop to Annie's daily visits to the lighthouse (65). "I never saw the Red Girl again," she states, "but I dreamed . . . [that] I took her to an island where we lived together forever" (71). In the end, the all-powerful mother discovers the "betrayal," and she kills the union that has cemented the girls' deep bond. Once again Annie sees her mother as a carrier of death, as someone who kills her relationship with the Red Girl and engenders a sense of loss and mourning.

This loss is also expressed in the autobiographical essay that Annie writes and presents to her class. Here Annie describes going swimming with her mother and losing track of her mother's location. Annie panics at the sudden loss but then glimpses her mother off in the distance, sitting on a rock in the sun. Annie, who cannot swim, is unable to get to her mother and her cries go unheard. Only her mother has the power to reestablish the connection (by returning to the shore), and Annie weeps until her mother swims back and comforts her by telling her daughter that she will never leave her again.

The essay is a metafictional moment in the text. Annie's composition of her autobiographical assignment reflects the overall

structure of the novel itself, in which Kincaid composes an autobiographical piece about her own separation from her mother.
In this scene, then, Annie is the talented, potential writer whom
Kincaid will eventually become. And according to the composition, Annie seeks to establish her identity outside of her
mother's circle of power, but she must do so in terms of the central conflict of her life, her troubled relationship to her mother.
Indeed the essay can be read as Annie's early attempt at finding
a voice of her own—a voice that will be heard and express her
individuality. As such, the assignment is a source of power for
Annie; she is able to gain respect by writing a text that becomes
the object of "adoration." After all, Annie's ability to use language impresses her classmates, and she becomes admired as a
"very bright" girl (37). But Annie's story has such an impact
because it speaks to the fears of the other girls in her class. They,
too, are anxious about losing the harmonious relationships that
they have with their mothers. Though Annie's story ends with a
lie, her fabricated conclusion calms the anxieties of her classmates and reassures them that they will not lose the love of their
mothers.

In the last few chapters of *Annie John*, Kincaid depicts the last
gasp of the mother-daughter relationship. Here Annie and her
mother are acknowledged enemies, engaged in a battle over
"what kind of woman" Annie will become. But Kincaid also
links this power struggle to the colonial situation of Antigua.
Indeed, symbolically speaking, a connection is drawn between
the "mother country" of the colonizer and the infantilized state
of the colonized nation. European dominance within a colonial
framework, then, mirrors the mother-daughter disharmony as
well as the shifting patterns of rebellion and dependence. Both of
these sources of power (the mother and the colonizer) are represented as limiting to the growth and subjectivity of the individual.

Annie, for instance, describes a history class in which she is taught to revere and mythologize European figures (such as Christopher Columbus) who were responsible for the colonization of Antigua and the spread of slavery throughout the Americas. This practice of the colonial school system makes the students very confused and disrupts a clear sense of identity. For Annie and the other children know that they are the descendants of those enslaved by the British, but at the same time they are taught to empathize with the British colonial project. On the one hand they seek to condemn the British for the crimes of the past, but on the other hand they are forced to salute the Union Jack and "swear allegiance" to England (115). "It was hard for us," Annie states, "to tell on which side we really belonged—with the masters or the slaves—for it was all history, it was all in the past. . . . [We] celebrated Queen Victoria's birthday. . . . But we, the descendants of slaves, knew quite well what had really happened" (76).

Annie is able to see this conflict early in her life. Her response is to reject the version of history disseminated at her school—a historical narrative that champions the European explorers who "discovered" the Caribbean. This rejection is expressed when she finds a color picture of Columbus in her history book. The picture is meant to inspire pity in the student—Columbus is being sent back to Spain in chains—but Annie sees the image as a depiction of justice. In the picture, Columbus is in the "bottom of the ship" and "bound up in chains" as he is being sent back to Spain after a decree from Bobadilla, a representative of the Spanish royal family. Annie believes that Columbus is getting his "just deserts," and she captions the picture with the words that her mother has used to describe her own overbearing but now feeble father: "The Great Man Can No Longer Get Up and Go"

(78). Annie's retitling of the picture in "old English script" expresses her desire to rewrite history. For Annie's words offer a different narrative to that which is put forward in her history book; her "rewriting" captures the justice of the punishment that Columbus must undergo. As a result, Annie is able to reframe the image and call attention to the fact that the picture echoes the history of the middle passage. After all, Columbus is placed in the same position as those Africans who were captured by Europeans and chained in the bottom of ships as they were transported to the Americas as slaves. Annie thus draws a connection between Columbus's "discovery" of Antigua and the violent history of slavery in the "new world."

Columbus, then, is not portrayed as a hero but as a tyrant. He is linked to an overbearing parent (her mother's father), and instead of "creating" Antigua with his "discovery," he is presented as a key figure in the destructive force that has crippled the island. The spread of European empire, Annie implies, has shrouded the Caribbean in darkness, turning it into a lost paradise. As such, Annie demythologizes the "official" colonial history and challenges national metanarratives that perpetuate social control through an exertion of imperialist ideologies. If these manipulative stories continue to dominate the island, then the country will remain in a constant state of dependence on the "mother country," never able to mature and develop a sense of identity separate from the colonial power. But Annie's teacher reads the act of retitling the picture as an unforgivable act of defacement. From the teacher's perspective, Annie has committed a blasphemy against one of the sacred men of history. The teacher, then, punishes Annie, quite ironically, by demanding that she copy out the first two books of John Milton's *Paradise Lost*.

The image of the overbearing parent is of course often associated with Annie's mother. But toward the end of the narrative, Annie's bond with her mother suffers its final death. The last, impassible rift occurs after Annie's mother has seen her daughter speaking with boys on the street. The scene develops when Annie is walking home from school. She is spotted by a group of four teenage boys, who begin to taunt her in a sexually suggestive manner. "I knew instantly," Annie states, "that it was malicious and that I had done nothing to deserve it" (95). She recognizes one of the boys and greets him in a friendly way. However, the other boys "whisper" in the background and "make fun of her" until she feels "ashamed" and turns away (99–100). This is an important moment for Annie, for it is an experience that drives home the injustices of gender difference. She has, as she points out, done nothing to solicit this disrespect. But it is thrust upon by the simple fact that she is "a big girl now" (99). She is thus, under the tyranny of the male gaze, defined as a sexually available object and humiliated by the experience. She returns home in a state of confusion, seeing herself as "alternatively too big and too small" (101).

Annie's pain finds no relief at home. Instead her mother inflicts a deeper wound when she says that she has watched Annie in town making "a spectacle of [her]self in front of four boys" (102). Her mother then calls Annie "a slut" (reminiscent of the short story "Girl") and condemns her daughter for being sexually transgressive until Annie retorts, "Well, like father like son, like mother, like daughter" (102). Annie decides to fight back—a decision that cements the divide between them.

Yet Annie's silencing of her mother is not a triumph. For Annie's experience engenders an awareness that her maturing body can be used as a weapon against her, both by the boys who mock her and by the mother who calls her a slut. This is a particularly painful stage in her personal development. Annie comes to realize that, within this society, a woman's body can impede her development by forcing her into an inferior role. Like the rape victim who is blamed for the crime, Annie is charged with an offence that she has not committed. The boys are not held responsible for their disrespectful behavior; instead she is blamed for an offence that she has not committed. The injustice of the situation is brought home to her. Annie's mere presence in public—as a young woman—is enough to solicit humiliating remarks and, in turn, she is condemned for the very comments over which she has no control.

Annie now takes her first steps toward leaving Antigua. She asks her father to build her a new trunk to replace the one that her mother brought to the island when she left Dominica. And she begins to see her mother's shadow as casting darkness over her life. Although she knows that her mother will always partly overshadow her, Annie also knows that she must leave her "mother land," otherwise the maternal shadow will cause her to wilt and die.

But before she leaves, Annie goes through what she calls her long period of illness. At his stage in her life, she falls into a deep pit of depression and suffers from a complete mental and physical collapse. She describes herself as being connected to the darkness of the "long rain" (the rainy season) and, upon looking inside her head, she finds a "black thing" lying there, shutting out all of the memories of her life (111). Her parents do not know what to do. Her mother takes her to see Dr. Stephens and then, when that does not work, she calls in an obeah woman, Ma Jolie, to perform certain rituals and to administer specific oils, waters, and sachets. But neither the European medicine nor the Caribbean obeah offer an immediate cure. Then one day, when her mother leaves the house to buy fish, Annie, in a state of delirium, collects all of the family photos in her bedroom and begins to wash them. She scrubs the photos so that, in one picture, she erases her mother and father from the waist down. In another photo, a wedding picture, she rubs out everyone's face except her own. Finally she washes the image of herself from her own confirmation photo, leaving only the representation of her shoes intact (120).

Annie's act of cleaning the pictures literally effaces her family and erases images that document the history of her life. Similar to her "defacement" of the picture of Columbus, Annie seeks to, once again, rewrite history. But here it is the history of her own family that she wants to change. By erasing the pictures, Annie tries to blot out the past and wipe the slate clean. She tries to forget the history of betrayal and hypocrisy that she now associates with her parents. And she wants to begin again, to reconstitute herself as a new person, by distancing herself from her past.

With the receding rain and the mysterious appearance of her grandmother, Ma Chess, Annie starts to come back to life. Perhaps her recovery is the result of Ma Chess's obeah magic (which is said to be much more powerful than that of Ma Jolie). Or perhaps it is just that the rain has simply washed everything away and left behind a place for her to grow. Whatever the case may be, Annie comes out of her "illness" as a new person. Her body has grown "to a considerable height" (she now "towers over" her mother), and she no longer fits into her old bed (128). She has found a new voice ("I acquired a strange accent") that is unique and strange ("no one had ever heard anyone talk that way before"; 128). To match her new body, Annie decides to make new clothes. In so doing, she has her new school uniform made to cover her entire body, choosing a long shirt that hides her legs and a hat with a "big brim" so that she can cover her face (128). If her body can be used as a weapon against her, she seems to suggest, then she is going to keep it under wraps. Her new identity is accompanied by a knowledge of the world, a loss of innocence, and a recognition of gender difference.

Annie then decides to leave the island. "The road for me now," she says, "went only in one direction: away from my home, away from my mother, away from my father" (134). She states that she never wants to "lie in [her] bed again"; she never wants to be woken up by her mother again; and she never wants to live under the "everlasting hot sun" of the island again (131, 134). She also admits that she does not necessarily want to travel to England and become a nurse, but she sees this as the best way to escape from her family and Antigua: "I did not want to go to England, I did not want to be a nurse, but I would have chosen going off to live in a cavern and keeping house for seven unruly men rather than go on with my life as it stood" (130). She knows that this departure will be permanent; she will never return to live on the island of her youth. But she also knows that she will take part of her family and the island with her, including her name.

On the "morning of the last day I spent in Antigua," Annie wakes up thinking, "My name is Annie John" (130). Here Annie articulates her identity, her sense of self, by uttering her name and asserting her autonomy. Annie claims her name for herself— a name she shares with her mother—and uses it as a way of defining who she is. This might be the island that formed her, but this is her last day here. She will thus leave and find a place where she can be herself, even while recognizing that Antigua has played an important role in the development of her subjectivity. Annie's departure might be final; she says that she will never return. But she also knows that, like her mother, who left Dominica at the same age, she will take part of her home along with her. Perhaps she can define herself elsewhere, but she will always take her name wherever she goes. The novel, then, concludes by echoing a statement that Kincaid has made about her own self-imposed exile: "What I really feel about America," she said, "is that it's given me a place to be myself—but myself as I was formed somewhere else."[6]

Lucy

Lucy (1990), Kincaid's highly acclaimed second novel, is, among other things, a continuation of *Annie John*. Although the name of the protagonist has changed from Annie to Lucy, Kincaid's second novel begins where her first novel ends: *Annie John* concludes with a departure, and *Lucy* begins with an arrival. In fact, the opening scene of *Lucy* depicts the first-person narrator, a teenager from Antigua, arriving in an unnamed American city. And yet it would be too limiting to read *Lucy* as a mere sequel to *Annie John*. For while the two books are similar in some ways, they are also very different in others. In terms of style and structure, for instance, the novels are quite distinct. *Annie John* is lush and descriptive, whereas *Lucy* is much sparser and more fragmented. *Annie John* tends to move chronologically through the events of the child's life, underscoring major themes with imagery and metaphor, whereas the narrative of *Lucy* resists chronology, moving back and forth in time while also avoiding clear-cut resolutions or conclusions. Moreover, the main character of each novel is unique. Annie is lively, curious, and engaged, whereas Lucy is more thoughtful, pensive, and critical.

The first-person narrative of *Lucy* is an account of the protagonist's life away from home, and her disorientation in this unfamiliar place. But her story is not just about the culture shock of immigrating to a new country; it is, more specifically, a meditation on what it means to "belong" and the psychological space between leaving and arriving. After landing in a city resembling New York, the central figure of the novel takes a job as a nanny for a wealthy, white American family. Her story opens with a description of her first day on the job, her surroundings, and her ambivalence about being away from home. Coming from a different cultural background, Lucy sees behind the happy facade of her privileged family that has employed her. She is able to compare this family with her own and make significant judgments based on her position as an "outsider." As she matures, Lucy's insights become increasingly complex, and her actions and mannerisms respond accordingly. This causes her to reflect upon the mental anguish that arises as she tries to detach herself from her homeland and distance herself from her own family. She, like Annie, has a complicated love-hate relationship with her mother. And as she builds a new life for herself outside of her "motherland," Lucy's strong voice and individuality emerge in the formation of a character who is defined by complexity and strength.

The initial reviews of *Lucy* were generally positive. However, one reviewer for the *New York Times* was disturbed by the disparity between Annie and Lucy, commenting that Lucy was too "disengaged" and "angry" compared with the highly "engaged" and "energetic" Annie.[7] Indeed, with Lucy, Kincaid develops what many critics will later refer to as her "angry" tone. But not all critics saw this as a negative development. Jeremy Taylor's article in *Caribbean Beat*, "Looking Back in Anger," suggests that Lucy's angry voice is important for the "repossession of self and the assertion of independence in the face of dehumanizing history." He also points out that Kincaid has dismissed some of her early work—particularly her first short stories—as too "unangry" and "decent," the sort of thing that "English people" wanted her to write: "I would never write like that again," she said.[8]

Lucy has also attracted the attention of many scholars within the field of literary studies. Her second novel appeals to an intellectual climate that is drawn to fiction that can be categorized as "transcultural," "postmodern," "black," "feminist," and "postcolonial." In 2002, for example, the highly respected academic journal *Callaloo* devoted a special issue to Kincaid's writing, and many of the articles focused on, or at least dealt with, *Lucy*.[9] In addition, the well-known literary critic Gayatri Chakravorty Spivak has lectured on, and written about, *Lucy* on a number of occasions. Spivak's preface to *A Critique of Postcolonial Reason* identifies *Lucy* as a significant work, for it, Spivak argues, demands the "right/responsibility of loving, denied to the subject that wishes to choose agency from victimage."[10] *Lucy* is, in other words, a kind of "success story" because it offers readers a migration narrative wherein a postcolonial subject can be empowered in a metropolitan environment.

Lucy arrives in the northern United States in the middle of January. Her feelings of dislocation and estrangement are thus reflected in the weather; she feels "cold and alien" in this strange and wintry land.[11] In fact, she describes her confusion at discovering that the weather can remain cold even when the sun is shining. "It was all wrong," she states, "The sun was shining but the air was cold" (5). Her basic assumptions about her new environment are thrown into doubt. She must start from scratch and learn about the basic characteristics of this new place. As a result she feels lost, and the blank whiteness of the snow begins to reflect her feelings of estranged bleakness in this unfamiliar and unpredictable place.

Lucy has sought to escape the strictures of life in Antigua. But she does not find an immediate sense of release or freedom in the United States. Rather she experiences a bewildering sense of alienation as she begins to realize "how uncomfortable the new can make you feel" (4). From the opening pages, Lucy's arrival is not represented as a comforting embrace that enables her to escape from her past life. Her disorientation in the new city forces her to come face-to-face with her past, and she must acknowledge that what she has learned in one cultural context is not transferable to another.

Lucy thus finds herself in an "in-between" state. She does not want to identify with her home in Antigua, but she does not experience a sense of belonging in the United States. She then becomes aware of the various juxtapositions that structure the world around her. For instance, she begins to see how Americans distinguish between "north" and "south," "black" and "white," "Western" and "non-Western." And she begins to recognize how these sets of oppositions have a profound impact upon people's worldviews as well as the way she is treated by the people around her. Moreover, she does not want to choose between identifying herself as a "Caribbean" person or as an American. Instead she wants to remain fluid rather than fixed, and she refuses to be tied to a specific place.

Lucy's "in-between" state is foregrounded when she receives a letter from her mother. The letter is "filled with detail after detail of horrible and vicious things" that her mother has heard about American cities (20–21). Her mother's letter affects the way in which Lucy sees the world; after reading this letter, Lucy says, "I was afraid to even put my face outside the door" (20).

Indeed the letter has reminded Lucy that she is in a strange place and that she is an immigrant, a long way from the comfort and safety of home. Lucy is, then, forced to reflect upon the difficulties of ever feeling at home in this violent and alien metropolis. But the letter also reminds her of the violence that she associates with her mother's powers of manipulation. If she were to return to Antigua, she would go back to an unhomely place with an overbearing mother who seeks to control her life. She thus places her mother's letter inside her brassiere and carries it with her wherever she goes, "not from feelings of love and longing . . . [but] from a feeling of hatred" (20).

One of the ways that Lucy tries to make sense of her situation is by defining herself as an exile. In a pivotal moment in the text, Lucy likens herself to one of the most famous modern-day European exiles, the painter Paul Gauguin. Lucy sees this Frenchman as someone who never felt comfortable in his native land and who traveled over vast distances in search of a sense of belonging. Concerning Gauguin, Lucy states, "I immediately identified with the yearnings of this man; I understood finding the place you are born in an unbearable prison and wanting something completely different from what you are familiar with, knowing it represents a haven" (95). But Lucy's identification with Gauguin is loaded with irony. For Lucy soon realizes that Gauguin's situation was quite different from her own. After all, he was a white European man; she is a black woman from Antigua. As a result, Gauguin's rejection of his Western home, his rebellion and exile, give him the "perfume of a hero," whereas Lucy's displacement will not be seen as heroic. "I was not a man," she says, "I was a young woman from the fringes of the world, and when I left home I had wrapped around my shoulders the mantle of a servant" (95).

However, the figure of Gauguin in Lucy's self-development is significant. For Gauguin offers the mythic narrative of the disaffected European who dismisses "civilization" and travels to the South Pacific in search of "primitive" and exotic cultures. Gauguin thus sets up a series of oppositions between the ideas of "civilized" and "noncivilized," European and non-European, white and black. Lucy soon becomes aware that Gauguin's worldview places her in the category of the exotic Other, a category that offered Gauguin creative inspiration and artistic self-definition. Lucy resists being cast in this role of Otherness, and she finds that the liberation experienced by Gauguin during his exile is not necessarily available to her in the United States. Here she will be seen as a "servant," and she must battle white perceptions of her blackness, foreignness, and exoticism in order to forge her own sense of self.

Lucy also distinguishes her own narrative from Gauguin's by calling attention to her gender. She sees that perceptions of her identity are not only determined by her "foreignness," but they are also established by the fact that she is a woman. Her body, then, defines her in specific ways, and she comes to realize that this gender difference means that she cannot hold the same privileged position as a man like Gauguin. She can, of course, use her body to gain a sense of sexual empowerment. But her body can also be used against her, marginalizing her in significant ways.

But it is also important to remember that Lucy's gender identity emanates from home and from her troubled relationship with her mother. For although Lucy has escaped from the overwhelming power of her mother, the maternal figure still holds a dominant place in her mind. After leaving home, Lucy finds that her mother's power seems, at times, to grow stronger. And she even begins to view her mother as God-like and omniscient, an ever-present and all-powerful being. In fact, her mother's power is so strong that Lucy refuses to open any more of her mother's letters. "If I read one," she states, "I would die from longing for her" (91).

Lucy's feelings about her mother pull her in two different directions. She sees her mother as the great love of her life and as the figure she must separate herself from if she is to develop her own identity. Lucy, then, views maternal love as something that threatens to kill her through suffocation. "I had come to feel that my mother's love for me was designed solely to make me into an echo of her; and I didn't know why, but I felt that I would rather be dead than become just an echo of someone" (36). If she is to grow into a complete individual, Lucy must distinguish herself from her mother. But Lucy finds it difficult to extricate herself from the maternal bond, and her journey to America—her rejection of Antigua—does not sever the link that she has with her past. "I used to think," she confesses, "that just a change in venue would banish forever from my life the things I most despised. But that was not to be so. As each day unfolded before me, I could see the sameness in everything; I could see the present take a shape—the shape of the past" (90).

This point is expanded upon when Lucy states, "My past was my mother" (90). Clearly her biggest obstacle to finding a new life in a new land is her intense bond with her mother—a bond that cannot be broken. Her mother is an extension of herself, and Lucy is an extension of her mother. Even when the maternal figure betrays the daughter, the connection is not completely severed. Lucy articulates such a betrayal when she describes the birth of her three brothers. An only child until the age of nine, Lucy has had her mother to herself for almost a decade. But after the birth of her first brother, Lucy watches as her mother's attention shifts away from the daughter to the son. The male child, that is, becomes privileged, and Lucy's mother imagines that her son will occupy an important and influential position in society. This same high position is not imagined for Lucy, and instead her mother pushes Lucy to become a nurse. Lucy identifies these different visions and expectations as a betrayal because her mother reinscribes a gender hierarchy that positions the son in the role of greatness and the daughter in the role of servitude. Lucy articulates this quite clearly when she states the following about her mother: "Whenever I saw her eyes fill up with tears at the thought of how proud she would be at some deed her sons had accomplished, I felt a sword go through my heart, for there was no accompanying scenario in which she saw me, her identical offspring, in a remotely similar situation" (130). Yet Lucy's belief in the continuity of past and present will not allow her to divorce herself from her mother, the woman she now secretly calls "Mrs. Judas" (131). For Lucy acknowledges that the present takes the shape of the past; the daughter takes the shape of the mother, and therefore physical separation is not enough. She cannot find "rebirth" through exile in America.

Lucy also witnesses the past repeating itself in her relationship with Mariah, her American employer. Mariah has a very different background from Lucy: she is white, American, wealthy, and privileged. However, at the beginning of their relationship, these differences do not impede the development of a strong bond between them. In fact, on the surface, Mariah is loving and affectionate with Lucy, welcoming her into the family as if Lucy were one of her own children. Mariah comes across as a kind and benevolent woman, and her affection and generosity for Lucy place her in the role of a mother substitute. For instance, soon after she begins to live with this family, Lucy states, "Mariah said to me, 'I love you.' And again she said it clearly and sincerely, without confidence or doubt. I believed her, for if anyone could love a young woman who had come from halfway around the world to help her take care of her children, it was Mariah" (26–27).

But Lucy soon starts to see cracks in Mariah's love. And she comes to understand that Mariah's love is not sincere; instead it is part of Mariah's exertion of power and authority. Lucy comes to this realization early in their relationship, for Mariah really wants Lucy to become a duplicate of her. "Mariah wanted all of us, the children and me," Lucy states, "to see things the way she did" (36). Mariah, then, wants Lucy to become an "echo" of her, to see the world through her privileged, American eyes, not her own. Lucy locates Mariah's hypocrisy in her hollow expressions of love—expressions that do not communicate a desire to have Lucy grow up and develop her own individuality. In the end, Lucy can see through Mariah because she has had a similar experience with her own mother.

And yet Lucy's relationship to Mariah is complicated. For although she sees Mariah's limitations, Lucy also states that "Mariah was like a mother to me, a good mother" (110). In fact, Mariah encourages Lucy's intellectual growth, buying her books and a membership to a museum. And while her own mother has been obsessed with preventing her daughter from becoming a "slut," Mariah takes for granted Lucy's need for sexual expression and provides Lucy with contraceptives. In addition, Mariah dislikes Lucy's cynical friend Peggy, but at the same time she accepts Lucy's need for this friendship. In this way, Lucy says, "Mariah was superior to my mother, for my mother would never come to see that perhaps my needs were more important than her wishes" (63–64).

The problems that arise between Lucy and Mariah are based on Mariah's refusal to recognize the differences between them. That is, Lucy is aware that Mariah's love and affection for her stem from her employer's "goodness" and generosity, but they also arise from her need to ignore (and thus erase) the profound cultural, racial, and economic differences that have defined their lives. Mariah chooses to remain blind to the inequalities that exist between her own privileged position and Lucy's position as her domestic servant. This means that Mariah is not sensitive to the power dynamics of class and race that she both maintains and perpetuates. Lucy knows that Mariah's lack of sensitivity and her complicity are based on the fact that "things have always gone her [Mariah's] way, and not just for her but for everybody she has ever known . . . she has never had to doubt . . . [because] the right thing always happens to her; the thing she wants to happen happens" (26).

Lucy has had a very different life from Mariah. This has equipped her to see what her employer cannot see, while maintaining a critical distance from privileged Mariah's life. The distance between them grows increasingly apparent as Lucy recounts her childhood in Antigua, telling Mariah stories from her youth. In one passage, for instance, Lucy tries to explain her colonial education to Mariah by speaking about how she was forced to memorize and recite William Wordsworth's poem about daffodils. Daffodils, Lucy explains, do not grow in Antigua, and yet the children in her school were expected to memorize a poem about flowers that were unknown to them—a poem written by a white man from England who had no connection to the island. Lucy uses this story to try to convey the power dynamics of her childhood, as well as the sense of cultural dislocation that she experienced growing up in the shadow of the British empire.

But Mariah cannot understand the story. She is, of course, sympathetic. But her response is to take Lucy to her favorite garden, blindfold her, and then reveal the splendor of a field of daffodils, thinking that the beauty of the flowers will erase Lucy's ugly association with the daffodils. Mariah seeks to gloss over cultural differences by imposing a universal model of aesthetics. From Mariah's perspective, the natural and timeless beauty of the daffodils can overcome social distinctions and place Lucy in a position from which she can see the world in the same light as her employer. Mariah, in effect, insists upon an apolitical view of the world that ignores the hierarchies and inequalities that have been established in the past. She does not recognize that history might determine the way in which Lucy looks at her environment, the way she sees a daffodil. And it is Mariah's shortsightedness that arouses Lucy's anger: she wants to lash out against Mariah and "kill" all of the flowers in the garden with an "enormous scythe" (29).

Nature is very important for Mariah, and she believes in environmental protection policies. But Lucy is aware that Mariah's commitment to environmental preservation only goes so far; Mariah is not willing to give up the comforts of her daily life in order to further the cause of conservationism. Indeed Mariah is a member of an environmental organization called "vanishing things." But Lucy insists that all of the wealthy members of this group are unable to make a connection between their own lives of consumption and the decline of the environment that surrounds them. Once again Lucy exposes Mariah's hypocrisy by indicating that her employer does the very thing that she condemns in others.

But the permanent break between them arises when Mariah tells Lucy that she (Mariah) has some "Indian blood" (39). Here

Mariah is once again trying to erase differences between herself and Lucy. As a result, her claim to have "Indian blood" is an attempt to make a connection to Lucy based on the bond of ethnicity and marginalization. But Lucy dismisses this bond: "To look at her, there was nothing remotely like an Indian about her" (40). What Lucy means by this is not just that Mariah does not have the physical appearance of a North American native; she also means that Mariah has always lived a wealthy Euro-American life and, as a result, she has never suffered from a history of colonization or disenfranchisement. This time, for Lucy, Mariah's hypocrisy leads to a fundamental contradiction: how can someone claim the identities of both the European victor and the defeated Indian? Mariah wants to have it both ways; she wants to live the privileged life of the victorious European American, while at the same time claiming to be connected to a vanquished band of Native Americans. "How can you get to be the sort of victor," Lucy asks, "who can claim to be the vanquished also?" (41).

The lack of communication between Mariah and Lucy becomes a barrier to their mutual understanding. However, Lucy's attitude toward Mariah changes as her employer's life begins to unravel. For as Lucy witnesses the breakdown of Mariah's marriage to Lewis, she begins to adopt a protective attitude. Mariah's simple and sunny view of the world makes it impossible for her to see what is happening right under her nose: Lewis is having an affair with Dinah, his wife's best friend. Lucy states that "Mariah did not know that Lewis was not in love with her anymore" because "it was not the sort of thing she could imagine" (81). In fact, Mariah's protected and rosy life has made her unsuited for this situation. By contrast, Lucy's view of the world enables her to see exactly what is happening between Dinah and

Lewis. "A woman like Dinah," Lucy states, "was not unfamiliar to me, nor was a man like Lewis. Where I came from, it was well known that some women and all men in general could not be trusted in certain areas" (80). As Lucy watches the affair develop, her sympathy for Mariah begins to grow, and she positions herself as Mariah's supporter and protector. Lucy, for instance, chooses to shield Mariah from the affair; she knows that if she tells Mariah about Lewis's infidelity she will only be responsible for inflicting more pain and suffering upon Mariah. Instead Lucy fosters a hatred for Lewis, who begins to manipulate Mariah into believing that she is responsible for the breakdown of their marriage.

These images of secrets and miscommunications are linked to the text's central metaphor, the tongue. Chapter 2 is even titled "The Tongue," and this part of the human body is used as an extended metaphor to explore issues of language and sexuality. For as Lucy struggles to come to terms with her new environment, she also struggles to find her tongue. She must, in other words, find a new way of speaking (she must speak in a different tongue) that can be understood in the context of white North America. At first she finds herself unable to communicate with the people around her. She cannot articulate herself in the presence of Mariah's friends, and when she does utter words, she is often misunderstood. For instance, in the opening chapter, Lucy tells Mariah and Lewis about a dream she has had about the couple chasing her around the house. This innocent narrative, which mixes together images from *Alice's Adventures in Wonderland* and *The Wizard of Oz,* is not well received by the couple because they misunderstand Lucy's intention for recounting the dream. Lucy had simply wanted them to know that she "had taken them in," because she only dreams about "people who were very important" to her (15). But Mariah and Lewis become extremely uncomfortable while listening to Lucy's dream, and Lewis responds inappropriately by saying "Poor, poor Visitor" and, likewise, Mariah says, "Dr. Freud for Visitor" (15). Lucy becomes very confused. Not only is she unclear about why the couple has become so uncomfortable, but she also wonders about the identity of this "Dr. Freud" (15).

As she undergoes this process of learning to speak in a "foreign tongue," Lucy also risks becoming defined by her "foreignness," for she is threatened with the danger of being forced into the role of Other, someone who will always remain an outsider in the United States. In fact, at times she finds herself being objectified by people who do not regard her as a full subject but instead view her as an exotic woman from "the islands" (65). Dinah, for instance, projects stereotypes about racial and cultural difference onto Lucy—stereotypes that threaten to categorize and fix her in a position of marginality. Lucy must battle this process of objectification by finding her own tongue. In the end, the tongue, the tool of oral communication, must be used by the protagonist as a way of articulating, and thus forming, a sense of self outside of stereotypes. In short, Lucy must find her own voice—a voice that is appropriate for this particular context.

As she adapts to the United States, Lucy begins to recognize the power of her tongue. Her sharp critiques of Mariah, for instance, are empowering because they constitute both an assertion of individuality and a resistance to Mariah's attempts to force her into a particular position. In fact, Lucy's sharp tongue becomes a way, not only of contesting Mariah, but also a way to find the path toward self-definition as Lucy is able to carve out a space for herself and assert her subjectivity by critiquing the identities of the people around her.

This means that although Lucy has symbolically lost her "mother tongue," she is not completely powerless or voiceless. This is exemplified in the final chapter, appropriately titled "Lucy," in which the protagonist speaks about her name. Here she uses the power of her tongue to name herself and thus assert her own identity. In so doing, she recounts the story of how, as a young girl, she decided to take on a different name; she therefore renamed herself Enid and rejected her given name.[12] But her mother was furious by her choice of the new name, for Lucy has inadvertently chosen the name of someone who has tried to kill her mother in a jealous rage. This story is significant because Lucy's rejection of the name given to her by her mother is also a rejection of her mother's tongue. After all, her mother's tongue was responsible for first speaking the name that would identify Lucy. By dismissing her given name, then, the daughter questions the mother's power and authority, thus putting distance between them.

The power of the tongue is also explored in Lucy's reflections on sensuality and sexuality. At one point, for instance, Lucy remembers how she liked to eat "boiled cow's tongue served in lemon sauce" (44). But, Lucy thinks, the cow's tongue had no real taste: "it was the sauce that made [it] so delicious" (44). She connects this image to the memory of her discovery that a boy's tongue also lacks taste. "At fourteen," she states, "I had discovered that a tongue had no real taste. I was sucking the tongue of a boy named Tanner" (43). Here she takes a significant step forward in her sexual development, for she realizes that it is not the taste of a boy's tongue that is important—it is how it makes her feel that counts.

Lucy's sexual discoveries are tied to the development of her subjectivity; Lucy's self-definition arises out of a form of subjectivity that is grounded in her physical experiences. Lucy, for instance, rejects her mother's repeated warnings against becoming a "slut" by having a number of casual sexual encounters with young men in New York. This sexual exploration is yet another way for Lucy to distance herself from her mother and proclaim her individuality. In so doing, she even sends a letter to her mother describing her recent adventures, stating that "life as a slut was quite enjoyable, thank you very much" (128).

This letter, though, is more than just an act of rebellion. It is also an act of claiming her sexuality and not denying herself the sensual pleasure of physical contact. From Lucy's perspective, her mother is a woman who has always suppressed her own sexuality, and Lucy refuses to repeat what she sees as her mother's mistake. This point is brought home to Lucy when she receives the news of her father's death. As a young man her father, she thinks, had been extremely sexually active, fathering perhaps thirty children with numerous women. Her mother, by contrast, has never explored her sexuality and has chosen to marry this man only because he was old and would "leave her alone." In fact, when she describes her parents' marriage, Lucy says the following: "She [Lucy's mother] had someone who would leave her alone yet not cause her to lose face in front of other women; he had someone who would take care of him in his dotage" (81). For Lucy, these gender roles are unacceptable: "This is not a situation I hoped to take as an example," she asserts (81).

Lucy embraces her body. Her first sexual encounter in the city is with Mariah's brother, Hugh, whom Lucy finds attractive because of his appealing eyes, hands, hair, voice, and smell. The attraction is very physical, and she finds intense pleasure in their bond. After kissing Hugh, for example, Lucy states that she enjoyed herself beyond anything she had ever known. But she also makes it clear that her pleasure is not connected to love: "I was not in love," she says about Hugh, "I was just enjoying the experience" (66). As a result, Lucy sees the relationship as based on pleasure for pleasure's sake: the desire to touch and be touched. So, too, is it in Lucy's relationship with Paul, an artist whom she meets through her friend Peggy. Here Lucy champions the pleasures of eroticism. "What an adventure this part of my life had become," she says, "I had not known that such pleasure could exist, and, what was more, be available to me" (113).

Yet Lucy decides to remain detached from her lovers. She refuses to get emotionally involved with these men; instead she chooses to cultivate a cold distance, even while she is physically close to them. A good example of this movement from physical attachment to emotional distancing arises in her relationship with Hugh. When she decides to break up with him, her arms are locked tightly around his body and she is kissing him passionately: "And that was how I said good-bye to Hugh, my arms and legs wrapped tightly around him, my tongue in his mouth, thinking of all the people I had held in this way" (83). Here Lucy's kisses are accompanied by a withholding of information; she has not yet told Hugh of her decision to break off their relationship. Her tongue thus performs a double role: she uses it to express passion through her kisses while simultaneously refusing to use it to express her decision to leave him. Lucy, then, wields a certain amount of power to determine the future of their bond. She reserves the right to continue the relationship and develop their intimacy, or she can rupture their union by putting an end to it.

By the end of the novel, Lucy is living alone. She has left her job as the nanny to Mariah's children, and she is working as a receptionist for a photographer. In her new apartment Lucy has found a place for herself; she now has a room of her own—

a place where she can find herself in the solitude of a sheltered space. She has escaped from those who would like to force her to conform to a specific identity (Mariah and her mother), and although she will never be completely free of her mother, she has now carved out an area wherein she can grow. At this point Lucy begins to describe her development as a process of inventing herself through narration and the writing of her own story. "My life," she says, "stretched out ahead of me like a book of blank pages" (163). This way of seeing her life is reinforced by Mariah, who gives Lucy a "blood red" notebook with blank white pages as a parting gift (162). One night, while alone in her apartment, Lucy opens the notebook and writes out her full name: "Lucy Josephine Potter" (163). Here, as in *Annie John,* the protagonist claims her given name for herself. She not only accepts the name her mother has given her, but she also asserts her given name as an expression of identity—an identity that is connected to a specific past associated with the family name of Potter.

But what she has gained also reminds Lucy of what she has lost. And instead of offering her satisfaction, this reclamation of self sparks a craving for a love that is so great that she "would die from it" (164). Perhaps this statement signals a desire to return to a time before the loss of maternal love—before her mother's betrayal. Or perhaps it indicates a void at the center of Lucy's life that can never be filled. What is certain, though, is that her wish gestures toward a loss of self. So that even while Lucy expresses the need to establish an independent identity, she also articulates a desire to lose herself in love. She wants a love so strong that she will erase herself in it—a love that will rob her of life through death. This desire for erasure is represented in the final lines of the novel, for once Lucy has written down these words she is overwhelmed with "shame" (164). She then begins to weep, and the flood of emotion washes over her so that her tears begin to "blur" the words she has written in her notebook.

This conclusion highlights the difficulties of writing the self. Lucy sees her life as a narrative, but she also realizes that she is not always the author of her own text, for at times she is not in complete control of her life's narrative. Certain scenes are composed by other people or places. Her mother has, for instance, left an imprint on her, and thus her mother has written part of Lucy's life story by influencing her in various ways. Moreover, Lucy's gender and race are aspects of her identity that sometimes define her from the outside, particularly through stereotypes or prejudices. Antigua, too, is a place that has helped to define the way she sees the world, and it will always be part of her no matter how much she tries to deny it. Finally, the history of colonization has marked her, and she has been exposed to a colonial education system that has taught her many lessons that she must "unlearn." Her words, then, become blurred because Lucy's narrative of self-creation cannot be written on a blank page. She is aware that she has absorbed certain cultural values that have had a profound effect on her life's story. Yet the novel ends with the beginning of Lucy's attempts to write herself. The end is a new beginning, and the reader recognizes the complexities involved in the writing of one's own story.

CHAPTER 4

Nonfiction

A Small Place and *My Brother*

A Small Place

If *Annie John* and *Lucy* can be described as texts that mix fiction and nonfiction, then *A Small Place* (1988) must be described as a nonfictional text infused with powerful poetic language, highly charged symbolism, and complex metaphor. This eighty-page essay is split into four sections, and it combines social and cultural critique with autobiography and a history of imperialism to offer a powerful portrait of (post)colonial Antigua. In a forthright and lyrical style, Kincaid candidly explores the impact of slavery and tourism on the island where she grew up. The book speaks directly to the American and European tourists who journey to Antigua in search of the escapism offered by sun, sand, and the Caribbean Sea. For Kincaid, these travelers perpetuate the slavery and imperialism practiced by their forefathers—not by keeping blacks in bondage chains but by contributing to an economy that keeps Antiguans shackled to tourism. Kincaid thus sees the citizens of Antigua, formerly British subjects, as still caught up in the hierarchies of colonization and economic imperialism. The island is, she suggests, unable to move beyond its status as a colonial nation.

Published in 1988, *A Small Place* is unique in style and form. It does not include the dreamlike images of *At the Bottom of the River;* nor does it continue the modes of the humor and wit found in *Annie John*. What we have here is an expression of concern, discontent, and anger. The loss and ruin of Antigua (through exploitation and colonization) projects itself into the present, and Kincaid turns that loss into an emotional eruption of anger and rage. "Antigua," Kincaid writes, "was settled by human rubbish from Europe, who used enslaved but noble and exulted human beings from Africa . . . to satisfy their desire for wealth and power, to feel better about their own miserable existence, so that they could be less lonely and empty—a European disease."[1]

Passages such as this accounted for Robert Gottlieb's decision to not publish *A Small Place* in the *New Yorker*. He considered the tone to be too angry and hostile for the largely white audience of the magazine. Indeed, when Farrar, Straus and Giroux first published the essay as a book, a number of white reviewers attacked the piece for what they considered to be Kincaid's unjustified expressions of bitterness and anger. For instance, Alison Hill, writing in the *New York Times Book Review*, stated that the text was "distorted by anger" and "backs the reader into a corner."[2] And a reviewer for the *Times Literary Supplement* (London) argued that Kincaid's attack was misplaced; she suggested that Kincaid's condemnation of the British was inappropriate seeing as Antigua gained self-rule in 1967 and achieved the status of an independent nation within the Commonwealth in 1981.[3] Other reviewers, though, were much more positive. Writing in the *Black Issues Book Review*, for example, Milca Esdaille stated that "in masterfully lucid language . . . [Kincaid] draws you into her world, imbuing ordinary language with extraordinary textured and multilayered meaning."[4] And Diane Simmons writes that many of the negative reviewers misread Kincaid's "painfully frank portrait of the postcolonial Caribbean" because they only focus on the first section of the book and, as a result, they do not fully understand the work's emotional and political complexities.[5]

But the book's powerful message begins to unfold in the first section. Here Kincaid reflects on what it means to be a tourist in Antigua. She suggests that when the North American or European first arrives in this small place his or her first response is to experience a sense of relief through escape. The tourist is, she writes, relieved to have escaped his everyday life back home; for a short time he does not have to worry about work, laundry, or buying groceries. It is this distance, this spatial separation from home, that allows the middle-class traveler to relax and "feel free" (5). For Kincaid, though, this white tourist repeats the patterns of racial and cultural domination that can be traced back to the institutionalization of slavery and imperial rule. The tourist arriving in Antigua, she maintains, might feel some guilt (based on the history of exploitation and colonization), but this feeling is, more often than not, repressed so that the tourist can have a nice holiday. This repression, then, forces the visitor to gaze at the Antiguans as objects, not subjects: the tourist looks at the "picturesque natives," never seeing them as human beings. Kincaid seeks to turn the gaze around; she wants to stare at the tourist from the perspective of the Antiguan. In so doing, she represents the citizen of the island as a subject and displaces the objectifying looks back onto the "incredibly unattractive, fat, pastrylike-flesh" of the white tourist (13).

A Small Place brings together two significant aspects of Kincaid's literary project: the pain that arises from exposing the truth and the personal suffering that accompanies loss. The text does this by combining truth with loss as Kincaid reveals truth by describing the exploitation and loss that lies behind the happy front of Antigua's tourist industry. Such an approach interrogates

Britain's colonial legacy and the effects of history on the current government officials who, in turn, contribute to the cycle of poverty on the island. The first part of the book's four sections disrupts the tranquility, peace, and beauty of the tourist's experience in Antigua by describing the dark side of the island's main economy. Here the reader is offered a profound social critique of American and European conceptions of Caribbean Otherness as well as the unethical culture of consumption that fuels Western tourism. The second section is largely autobiographical. Here Kincaid presents various memories of her childhood in British-ruled Antigua. She describes her formation as a colonial subject—someone who was forced to internalize the cultural values and historical narratives imposed upon her by a colonial education system and a government that was controlled from London. Section three moves from the past into the present. Here Kincaid focuses her gaze on the problems with the current Antiguan government. She uncovers corruption, and she links the stunted values of government officials to a past that haunts the present. Section four, the final part of the book, describes the beauty of Antigua and the potential that *could* develop in this small place. There is, in the end, a guarded optimism, a slight ray of hope for the future.

The writing style of *A Small Place* is spare, incisive, often ironic, blunt, and even brutal. There is no escape from the pain Kincaid portrays and displays, and nowhere for her targets (the tourists, the British, the Antiguan government) to hide. This is, of course, one of the constant refrains of her writing: that there is nowhere to hide, nowhere to go, no shelter, no home, and no escape. Instead Kincaid suggests that people are forever bound together, and the task of the individual is to re-create those bonds that are humane and just. The tourist, as she portrays him, is unjust; he is embedded in an invisible web of exploitation that generates suffering and perpetuates loss.

In the first part of the essay, Kincaid interrogates the profound cultural differences confronted by the Western tourist who visits the developing country. For the tourist to enjoy his visit, he must fully accept the spatial distance between himself and the citizen of the country. The visitor must see himself as journeying to a place that is totally unrelated to the world he inhabits. Kincaid puts this quite clearly at the beginning of her text; she addresses the tourist directly and calls attention to the complete separation that is the source of freedom and renewal for the tourist. "You disembark from your plane," she writes, "You go through customs. Since you are a tourist, a North American or European—to be frank, white . . . you move through customs with ease. Your bags are not searched" (4–5).

Kincaid's antagonistic style of addressing the reader as "you" creates a distinction between the author and her readers. In fact, throughout the book the author describes "you"—the tourists— as "white," "ugly," "empty," "stupid," "fat," and "rubbish." On the surface, it might seem that Kincaid is participating in the same discourses of racism that she condemns in others—that she is painting all white people with the same brush. But when readers begin to scratch the surface, they start to see that Kincaid makes important distinctions between those whites who remain at home and those who become tourists. She also makes important cultural distinctions between white North Americans and Europeans. Such nuances move her accusatory tone outside of the realm of racism by indicating that the author's goal is not to attack all white people. Rather she seeks to attack the process by which some whites from North America and Europe become tourists and benefit from the exploitation of other people.

It is through her provocative language that Kincaid highlights power relations and the implications of such power. Readers are, for instance, forced to reflect upon where Kincaid's "you" places them. The author asserts that "you" never consider "that the people who inhabit the place in which you have just paused cannot stand you" (17). Here the "truth" of interpersonal relations and subject positions are exposed, and Kincaid's use of the second person singular strategically positions readers in her world. It is thus clear that Kincaid is not speaking to readers who share her opinion; she is not necessarily interested in writing for an audience that knows what she knows. Rather she seeks to enlighten those tourists who do not understand the implications of their visits or their privileged status within a global economy.

Kincaid then condemns the tourist for not being self-reflexive. The visitor is, she states, unable to situate himself in the context of the "small place," and as a result, he cannot see the humanity of the people he meets. Kincaid writes, "You see yourself taking a walk on that beach, you see yourself meeting new people (only they are new in a very limited way, for they are people just like you). You see yourself eating some delicious, locally grown food. You see yourself, you see yourself." (13). The repetition in this passage is striking: the tourist can only "see" himself. He is only concerned with the self-interest of seeking pleasure, and he lives in the moment in order to escape his unexamined life back home. Because the object of his journey is to satisfy his desires, the tourist is blind to the implication and impact of his vacation.

Kincaid, then, describes the typical day of the tourist: he eats in local restaurants, he suns himself on the beach, he goes swimming, and he watches the sunset. There are moments during his day when he sees flashes of how the local people live—they are poor, but their lives are perceived as simple, happy, calm, and uncluttered. The tourist, then, focuses on the differences between his life and the lives of the local people; he revels in the difference as a way of distancing himself from those he encounters. Similarities are few and far between. The tourist sees the Antiguans as having "their" own culture on their pretty Caribbean island, and this is juxtaposed to the busy, fast-paced life in the modern cities of America and Europe. This bustling modern world, "the real world," is back home in the metropolis of the developed world. Antigua is, by contrast, a pleasant and nice place for a holiday, but it is not "real." Rather it is a fantasy land that offers a moment of escape. From this point of view, the tourist can separate the Caribbean island from the powerful industrial nation of his homeland. He can therefore enjoy his vacation because he does not have to see his holiday, his escape, as part of an economic cycle of consumption that furthers the disparities between the rich and the poor. If the tourist is distanced from the scene before him, if he can separate himself from the island, then he can also convince himself that he is not responsible for the differences in economic privilege that constitute his relation to the Antiguan citizen.

But this separation and distancing also includes a hierarchy. The tourist sees himself as superior, for the differences between his life and the natives' lives are filtered through the gaze of the visitor. Despite the allure of the simple life, the tourist regards the Antiguan as premodern or even primitive. Still addressing the reader-as-tourist, Kincaid writes, "And you look at the things they [Antiguans] can do with a piece of ordinary cloth, the things they fashion out of cheap, vulgarly colored (to you) twine, the way they squat down over a hole they have made in the ground. . . . Their ancestors were not clever in the way yours were and not ruthless in the ways yours were, for then would it not be you who would be in harmony with nature and backwards in that charming way?" (16–17). It is at this point that the tourist is ready to go home. The European or North American city might not be as charming, it might not be in harmony with nature, but it is modern and advanced. It is more powerful—indeed, it is the center of power—and as such it represents, for the tourist, the center of civilization.

In the end, Kincaid suggests, the tourist begins to feel uneasy on the island. Perhaps this is based on the tourist's faint recognition that he is not liked by the citizens of Antigua. In fact, the native mocks the tourist behind his back. "The people who inhabit the place," Kincaid states, "cannot stand you . . . they laugh at your strangeness . . . they do not like the way you speak . . . they do not like you" (17). The tourist, then, starts to feel "out of place," and the sweetness of the island begins to turn sour. And yet the tourist cannot understand why this change has occurred, why he is not liked, so the distance and separation remains in tact as the visitor boards the plane to go home. For Kincaid, the story of the tourist encapsulates one particular way of understanding the relationship between places. The tourist goes to Antigua to experience a culture that is wholly contained within a geographically bound space. The tourist then leaves with the false belief that he has experienced the full life of Antigua. His self-deception is based on the fact that he has not forged any connections to this island. He has not become self-reflexive about his own complicity in the exploitation that arises out of his economic power and privileged status. He has not, in short, formed any meaningful link to the people from this place —a link that will cause him to change his perspective on the world or transform his lifestyle.

But the story of the tourist is not the only tale that Kincaid seeks to tell. She is, in fact, more interested in the people who are left behind—the Antiguans who remain on the island after the tourist has gone home. For Kincaid is able to see the connections between the lives of the tourists and the culture, politics, history, and economics of Antigua. Indeed what Kincaid illustrates is the way in which the experience of the tourist is intimately tied to the global economic system fueled by the North American or European metropolis that the tourist calls home. This global economy is illustrated in the very food that is eaten by the tourist while he is on the island. "When you sit down to your delicious meal," Kincaid writes, "it's better you don't know that most of what you are eating came off a plane from Miami. And before it got on a plane from Miami, who knows where it came from? A good guess is that it came from a place like Antigua first, where it was grown dirt-cheap, went to Miami, and came back" (14). Here Kincaid calls attention to the complex artifice of presenting the illusion of a local culture for the tourist. The "authentic" Antiguan food might or might not be produced in a developing economy (for which the local people would be paid very poorly) before it moves through global economic channels. Perhaps the food is grown in the Caribbean, but then it is processed in North America before it is sent back to Antigua to be consumed by the tourists. The transnational movement of food turns it into an expensive commodity—a commodity that the local people of Antigua cannot afford to buy. What lies behind Kincaid's comments, then, is a cutting irony: the local people cannot afford the very food that they grow.

This irony reveals the power structures that define the island, and it exposes the inequities between wealthy and poor nations. Antigua's poverty is further highlighted by the fact that it cannot afford a sewage system. Kincaid focuses on this and uses it to make yet another connection between life in Antigua and the lives of the tourists. "You must not wonder what exactly happened to the contents of your lavatory when you flush it. You must not wonder where your bath water went when you pulled out the stopper. You must not wonder what happened when you brushed your teeth. Oh, it might all end up in the water you are thinking of taking a swim in; the contents of your lavatory might, just might, graze gently against your ankle as you wade care free in the water, for you see, in Antigua, there is no proper sewage-disposal system" (13–14). There is, in this passage, an implied connection to the previously quoted passage. For Kincaid implies that the consumption of the transnational food will produce human waste that is not adequately treated. This waste is not properly dealt with because the transnational companies responsible for the processing of Antigua's produce keeps the island immersed in poverty so that Antiguans cannot afford a proper sewage system. And this situation could have a negative impact upon the tourist who wants to go for a swim, as well as on the general health of the environment.

The images of swimming and the beach arise throughout Kincaid's essay. This is not surprising when we consider that the beach is an integral part of Antigua's tourist industry, and it is therefore integral to the island's economy. The beach is a source of pleasure for the tourist, but Kincaid also shows how pleasure for some is pain for others. From this perspective, Antigua is not cut off from the rest of the world—it is not a fantasy world of fun and games. Instead it is a beach on which the multiple global dynamics of economic imperialism, injustice, poverty, despair, and hope are played out. Kincaid explores this point by showing that the culture seen by the tourist is scarred by the history of

British colonialism. Antigua is, she points out, a very new country: it became self-governing in 1967, and it achieved full independence within the Commonwealth in 1981. The scars of colonization, then, are still fresh, and Kincaid writes with first-hand knowledge about the negative effects of this power relation. Her experience growing up in a British-style education system meant that she, in her own words, grew to "detest everything about England, except the literature."[6] The colonists, Kincaid concludes, attempted to turn Antigua "into England" and the natives "into English" without regard for the local culture (24).

Colonization, then, is an important theme throughout *A Small Place*. Kincaid expresses her anger at the British, but she also attacks her fellow Antiguans for failing to fully achieve their independence. Part of her anger is fueled by the fact that she identifies the relationship between the colonizer and colonized in terms of an unhealthy power dynamic based on parent-child relations. In fact, Kincaid links colonization to a coercive and quasi-parental bond of one nation toward another. At one point, for instance, she writes about the English as if she is describing her mother's parenting style: "No natural disaster imaginable could equal the harm they did" (30). Such comments shed light on the underdeveloped state of the nation's independence. For Kincaid does not want to criticize Antiguans without first noting that their arrested development is, in part, the result of a dysfunctional and infantilized relationship to the colonizer.

One of the problems with Antigua is that, according to Kincaid, the citizens still perpetuate the traditions imposed upon them by the "mother" country. For instance, she writes that May 24th, Queen Victoria's birthday, is still a national holiday on the island. Instead of being angry over Queen Victoria's role in colonization, the population is grateful for the holiday from work. The citizens are neither self-reflexive about what the holiday symbolizes nor do they see Queen Victoria as a destructive mother figure who infantilized the nation. For Kincaid, in fact, Queen Victoria should not be celebrated, for she is a figure of destruction who should be held responsible for the loss of Antiguan culture. Kincaid points out that the original languages of the island are no longer spoken; they have been replaced by the "Queen's English," the language of the colonizer. "What I see," Kincaid writes, "is the millions of people, of whom I am just one, made orphans: no motherland, no fatherland, no gods . . . and worst and most painful of all, no tongue. . . . For isn't it odd that the only language I have in which to speak of this crime is the language of the criminal who committed the crime?" (31). Here Kincaid highlights the fact that Antiguans have no "mother" tongue to call their own. Instead they are forced to speak in the very language of the people who have ruled over them. As a result, this language is inadequate for expressing the criminal deeds perpetuated by the colonial power. For this language is built to express an Englishman's point of view, and thus it cannot adequately articulate the horror, injustice, and agony of colonization from an Antiguan perspective.

However, it is through an awareness of the history of colonization, Kincaid suggests, that one can understand Antigua's current situation. Tourism, that is, can only be understood in the context of a background of economically driven external intervention, for the imperialism of the nineteenth century is linked to the economic institutions of the late twentieth century. And the exploitation of Antigua is part of the driving force of trade that has always fueled the growth of European and American capital. Kincaid then uses the contemporary example of Barclays

Bank in order to illustrate her point. "The Barclay Brothers, who started Barclay's Bank," she writes, "were slave-traders. That is how they made their money. When the English outlawed the slave trade, the Barclay brothers went into banking. It made them richer. It's possible that when they saw how rich banking made them, they gave themselves a good beating for opposing an end to slave trading" (25–26). Here Kincaid connects the establishment and growth of a multinational bank to the nineteenth-century spread of slavery and colonization. Barclays Bank is, of course, an important financial institution in contemporary Antigua. But it is also one of the largest banks in the world, generating enormous annual profits for its managers and shareholders. In 2004, for instance, the worldwide pretax profits reported by Barclays Bank exceeded six billion U.S. dollars, more than nine times as much as the annual GNP of Antigua in that same year.[7]

The recent adaptation of *A Small Place* for the narrative of the film *Life and Debt* illustrates the ways in which Kincaid's text addresses globalization.[8] The film, a critique of global capitalism and multinational companies, uses *A Small Place* to highlight the continuing forms of imperialism that are perpetuated by lending agencies (such as the International Monetary Fund), the tourist industry, and unequal terms of trade. And yet it is Kincaid's vision of the past that makes her insights so powerful in the present: "Do you know why people like me are shy about being capitalists? Well, it's because we, for as long as we have known you, *were* capital, like bales of cotton and sacks of sugar, and you were the commanding, cruel capitalists, and the memory of this is so strong, the experience so recent, that we can't quite bring ourselves to embrace this idea that you think so much of" (36–37).

Antigua is, Kincaid argues, controlled by a world increasingly dominated by the United States and U.S.-based corporations, further complicating the dynamics of place and global relations. But it is not only the agents of globalization and imperialism whom she criticizes: Kincaid also places blame upon Antiguans themselves: she condemns the citizens of this small place for not being aware of history, and as a result, she criticizes the population for repeating the mistakes of the past. In the middle of the narrative, for example, Kincaid records her impressions of Antigua upon returning to the island after an absence of many years. In reference to the Antiguan youth, she states, "What surprised me most was how familiar they were with the rubbish of North America—compared to my generation, who were familiar with the rubbish of England—[and] . . . how unable they were to answer in a straightforward way . . . simple questions about themselves" (44). In this passage Kincaid indicates that the Antiguan youth are continuing an unhealthy pattern of inferiority and dominance that now locates the center of empire in North America rather than England. The past, then, is repeated in the present, for Antiguans are continuing to identify with the dominating culture that exploits them. But if the youth know about the "rubbish" of America, they do not know about themselves or the history and culture of their own island.

Kincaid does not let Antiguans off the hook. She claims that Antigua's citizens have failed to adopt the positive aspects of English culture—including an effective education system—and have chosen to take on the habits that do not better their lives. In addition, she argues, the government makes policies that do not help the population. For instance, the neglect of the education system is symbolized in the failure to rebuild Antigua's only library, which was "damaged in the earthquake of 1974" but still bears the sign "REPAIRS ARE PENDING" (9). Although it remains standing, the library building is not safe for the public. Kincaid thus uses the damaged building as a symbol for reflecting upon various aspects of contemporary life in Antigua, ranging from ignorance about history to corruption in the government. Indeed her description of the library is complex and conflicted. On the one hand, she feels a sense of loss when she considers the closure of the "beautiful" old building with its "open windows" and its "rows and rows of shelves filled with books" (42). The library—both the inside and the outside—is remembered fondly. On the other hand, Kincaid recognizes that the material housed in the library (a building constructed by the British) was meant as yet another tool of colonization: the holdings had the function of acquainting Antiguans with narratives and stories that promoted an idealized view of English history and society. The library's collection, Kincaid writes, disseminated the "fairy tale" of England as a benevolent nation that was nurturing the island (43). From this perspective, she states, the books are a source of lies that the English used to justify the imperialism project.

Yet the closure of the library is also a symbol of failure—the failure of Antigua to move forward in the wake of independence. Kincaid's description of the building leads her to criticize the rampant corruption in Antigua's government. Individuals in public office, she maintains, have been more interested in lining their pockets than promoting the public good. "The government is corrupt," Kincaid writes, and every Antiguan acknowledges this, saying "them are thief, them are big thief" (42). Thus the money that could be used to repair the old library and replace the old collection is not available; the nation's treasury has been pillaged by corrupt government officials. Consequently, a small number of the library's books have been moved to a temporary library, which Kincaid describes as a "dung heap" above a "dry-goods store in an old run-down cement-brick building" (42–43).

Corruption, then, is connected to the failure of education. And the failure of education is connected to a lack of historical awareness. Kincaid asserts that Antiguans are, not surprisingly, "obsessed" with slavery. But the population, she goes on to say, has a perverted sense of its history, and the people construct a historical narrative of slavery that describes "a pageant full of large ships sailing on blue water, the large ships are filled up with human cargo—their ancestors" (54). Slavery is, for Antiguans, the story of a dramatic performance, a pageant of costumes and props that is located in the realm of fantasy. This unreal story, Kincaid states, even extends to emancipation: "The word 'emancipation' is used so frequently, it is as if it, emancipation, were a contemporary occurrence, something everybody is familiar with" (55). Here Kincaid implies that the danger of the Antiguan story of slavery is in its distancing, for the narrative (which moves from the grandness of the ships to the beauty of the sea to the pain of victimization to the simple fact of emancipation) is not examined in relation to contemporary life on the island. The story is firmly fixed in the past, so that connections are not made to the present.

Kincaid concludes by suggesting that Antigua's alienation from its own history is self-destructive because this divide does not allow the citizens of the nation to make connections between their "obsession" with slavery and the contemporary tourist industry. Nor can they link colonization and the corruption of the government to the fact that foreign financial institutions continue to control the island's economy. Rather Antiguans prefer to see themselves as liberated and emancipated. And because their narrative of slavery is based on a fantasy, they do not fully understand their history: this means that, for Kincaid, they are doomed to repeat it. As an example of this repetition, she points to the Hotel Training School. This school has become the chief educational facility on the island, and Antiguans are proud of the institution (graduation ceremonies are even broadcast on television). But the main function of the school is to teach the Antiguan youth to become servants to the privileged tourists who visit the island. As a result, the white, wealthy foreigner continues to dominate this small place, forcing black Antiguans into positions of servitude.

History repeats itself. And it does so because Antiguans do not examine the forces of the past and the present that influence their lives. Kincaid's project is to intervene in that repetition. Her text is an attempt to break the unhealthy patterns of narrative construction in Antigua and offer a fresh view of the island that is not clouded by fantasy or fueled by delusion. But *A Small Place* does not speak only to Antiguans. The text also speaks directly to white readers about how colonization, slavery, tourism, and globalization are intimately intertwined. Thus Kincaid illustrates that North Americans and Europeans perpetuate the power dynamics that were established in the past and that continue to have negative effects upon the residents of her nation. More important, though, the text calls attention to how the continuation of these inequities is destructive for both the colonizer and the colonized. While the colonized group suffers from exploitation, poverty, and marginalization, the colonizers are caught up in perpetuating a vicious cycle of greed and consumption that causes a profound disconnect in their lives, displacing those at the center of power from ethics, morality, and humanity.

My Brother

In 1997 Kincaid published an autobiographical work titled *My Brother.* This memoir, which was nominated for a National Book Award for nonfiction, explores many of the issues and themes found in her earlier work. The book was inspired by the death of her brother, Devon Drew, from AIDS in 1996. Yet the narrative is also about Kincaid's own memories and impressions of her family in relation to her brother's illness. While much of the text describes Devon's suffering, large sections of the book are taken up with accounts of the author's conflicted and explosive relationship to her mother, Mrs. Drew. Moreover, as the narrative develops, many details emerge concerning Kincaid's life. She writes, for instance, about her home in Vermont and her own children; she writes about her relationship to her two other brothers, all of whom have a difficult relationship with their mother. She writes about her intense love for her husband, Allen Shawn; and she even describes herself as a keen gardener.

My Brother has been both praised and condemned by critics. Those critics who wrote negative reviews of the book tended to take Kincaid to task for writing what seems on the surface to be a biography of Devon but which is not only concerned with his life. Taking this perspective, Diane Hartman states that *My Brother* lacks focus: "It is hard to figure out why Kincaid wrote this book," Hartman writes in the *Denver Post,* "the book isn't a tribute or memorial [to Devon] and has no moral or discernible point."[9] Likewise, John Skow attacked Kincaid in *Time* for not writing enough about her brother's life; he argued that she selfishly indulged in writing about her own problems. As such, Skow refers to the narrative as an "irritating navel contemplation," in which Kincaid "repeats the pattern of familiar, well-written complaint."[10] Other critics were much more positive.

For instance, Anna Quindlen, writing in the *New York Times,* describes the memoir as a brilliant work "about the chasm between the self we might have been and the one that we have somehow, often inextricably, become."[11] Quindlen, unlike Skow, sees no problem with the distinction between the title and the content. Rather she identifies *My Brother* as a powerful portrait of life and death, leaving and becoming, familiarity and foreignness, as well as domesticity and alienation. Similarly, Sarah Kerr states that the memoir is a success because it describes rage in an elegant fashion but then ultimately moves beyond rage: "Rage is only one shade in the spectrum of human experience. Kincaid's new memoir is more expansive than her fiction—and at times more moving—because in it, she begins to explore some of the others."[12]

These comments on rage are insightful, for Kincaid has often been attacked for expressing anger and bitterness in her writing. But to see her work as moving beyond rage is consistent with the complex range of emotions that Kincaid weaves into all of her work. In fact, when an interviewer from *Mother Jones* asked Kincaid about those critics who have condemned her work as too angry, she replied that "whatever I say in my writing, in my personal life I'm really incredibly lucky. I suppose that's what gives me the freedom to express negatives."[13]

The structure of *My Brother* is nonlinear, and it is split into two sections. The first section begins with Kincaid's description of her visit to the Holberton hospital, where Devon is dying of AIDS. The narrative then suddenly moves from an account of the circumstances surrounding her brother's death to the events of his birth. Both stages of his life, Kincaid remarks, have taken place in a hospital, for Devon is the only one of Kincaid's siblings to have been born in a hospital ward. This thematic shift from death to life (as sparked by the setting of the hospital) is typical of the way in which the events of the narrative are presented to the reader. In fact, the strange logic of this leap only begins to make sense when we realize that the narrative follows the patterns of Kincaid's memory. As readers, then, we are confronted with the idiosyncratic flow of Kincaid's consciousness. Consequently the events of the narrative do not always unfold in a rational manner; instead they take a circuitous route though the processes of remembrance and contemplation.

Throughout the first section, Kincaid writes about how she has distanced herself from her family. But she also describes how her brother's illness pulls her back into the lives of her mother and brothers. Moreover, Kincaid's return to Antigua and her shifting proximity in relation to her family sparks a plethora of memories, ranging from painful experiences in her youth to her mother's belief in the dangers of obeah practice. In fact, as memories flood back to her Kincaid begins to reflect upon the strength of her memory. "When I was a child," she writes, "she [my mother] would look at me with wonder and pleasure and praise me for my extraordinary memory. . . . As I grew up, my mother came to hate this about me, because I would remember things that she wanted everybody to forget."[14] At one stage of her life, Kincaid's ability to recall events and situations is identified by her mother as an asset; at another stage, this same trait is condemned as a liability. For the daughter, the irrationality of this change is seen as a betrayal. But Kincaid also understands that this particular act of betrayal arises out of her mother's desire to ignore her own transgressions. She does not want her daughter to remember things because she does not want to be confronted with the negative aspects of herself. This gives rise to one of Kincaid's harshest critiques of her mother: Kincaid condemns her for having a selective memory and intentionally forgetting the mistakes of her the past. The author maintains that this act of forgetting has a purpose, for her mother can never admit that she has committed errors or caused others pain—she cannot, in other words, apologize or ask forgiveness, so forgetting becomes the only option.

My Brother, though, also includes many descriptions of Devon's life and death. Long passages are, for instance, devoted to his physical condition, his body, and his thoughts. Because Devon was only three years old when Kincaid left Antigua, she has not developed a close bond to Devon, and her memories of him are sometimes quite vague. However, her recollections of him are generally very positive, although she is also frank about his shortcomings. She describes him as an intelligent, well-read, attractive, charming, and athletic young man who has never been able to live up to his potential. He has been deeply troubled, and this has impeded his personal development. At age fourteen, Kincaid writes, Devon became involved in criminal activities. He was charged in a gas station robbery in which the attendant was murdered. Devon was tried, convicted, and sent to prison (24–25). But his jail sentence was reduced because he testified against his friends and his mother asserted her political influence. As an adult, he continued to break the law: Devon is described as stealing various items from his mother (taking one of her prized plants and selling it for money to buy drugs) and his brother, Joe (taking his expensive set of tools) (73). Devon's criminality is, according to Kincaid, a byproduct of his drug abuse, for she writes that he frequently took cocaine and smoked marijuana with his Rastafarian friends.

Still, Kincaid describes her brother as an extremely charming young man. In fact, Kincaid writes that the one good thing to come out of Devon's illness is the fact that she can now see his positive traits. Consequently she becomes aware of her deep love for him. She thus describes him as a brilliant person, albeit someone who has been impeded by his own damaged psyche. Had he been able to cope with his demons, she suggests, Devon could have made an important contribution to society. He could have become an influential public figure, for he had a talent for speaking to people in eloquent and moving ways. Devon, though, has never been able to develop his gifts because he could never recognize them in himself. "He was never remotely aware," Kincaid writes, "of such a person inside him. It was I who told him this . . . and I saw that he wished what I said was really true . . . wished he knew how to make the effort to make it true. He could not" (59–60). Instead Devon's low self-esteem causes him to lose himself in a fantasy world in which he daydreams he is "a famous singer" for whom "women remove their clothes" when they hear him sing (60). Here Kincaid sees her brother as a dreamer whose fantasies stop him from ever fully knowing himself. His daydreams are thus significant because they signal Devon's underdeveloped identity, and they suggest that he is stuck in an early stage of personal growth.

The reader's perception of Devon is not always as sympathetic as Kincaid's view of her brother. For Devon is a disturbing figure. When his AIDS virus goes into remission, for instance, he becomes convinced that he is cured. As a result, Devon's fantasies begin to dictate his actions. He starts to falsely believe that he can settle down and have a family, with "a woman bearing his own children" (57). He falsely believes that he can continue taking drugs and drinking without it having a negative effect upon his health. But what is most disturbing is that his self-fostered illusions about being cured inspire him to resume sexual relations without using adequate protection. "My brother," Kincaid writes, "had been having unprotected sex [with a nameless Guyanese girl] and he had not told her that he was infected with the HIV virus" (66). Devon, then, is perpetuating a vicious cycle of contagion. He has contracted the disease through unprotected sexual activities with partners who may or may not know that they have HIV. And yet the knowledge of his own condition does not prevent him from having unsafe sex with women who are unaware of his HIV status. Even more disturbing is the fact that he does not care about the health or well-being of his partners. Devon is not concerned about exposing other people to HIV, and he justifies his actions by saying simply that "he could not go two weeks without having sex," for "two weeks without sex makes [him] feel funny" (67).

Kincaid writes that Devon's views are shared by other men in Antigua. While her brother believes that his sexual desires are "unique" and that they make him a "powerfully sexual man," she writes that "every man" she has ever known has "said the same thing, two weeks without sex make them feel funny" (67). Moreover, Dr. Ramsey, one of the few Antiguan doctors who treats patients with AIDS, tells Kincaid that he often sees other HIV-positive men with similar ideas. He describes giving lectures on AIDS to men in St. John's, who go directly to prostitutes once a lecture is over. These men, Ramsey says, know that the majority of these prostitutes (the "butter women," light-skinned women from Santo Domingo) are infected with HIV. Still the men tell Dr. Ramsey that "they would rather die than leave the butter women alone" (39).

The first section of *My Brother* includes a political dimension. Kincaid describes the lack of education surrounding HIV and AIDS. She links this to the poor state of health care in Antigua, as well as the poverty that perpetuates unhealthy lifestyles. She tells of the unsanitary conditions of the Holberton hospital, where patients rarely get the correct treatment and thus remain ill. And she gives an account of how AIDS patients are treated with shame; they are often isolated in dirty sections of the hospital that are no longer in general use, and they do not receive proper attention or care. Seeing the hospital where Devon is treated, Kincaid is appalled. The furniture is old and broken, the ceiling fans are hazardous to the patients, and even basic medications such as aspirin are not always available. Moreover, the doctors and nurses consider AIDS to be a death sentence; they do not believe that, given the appropriate medicine, an HIV patient can recover and lead a relatively normal life. As a result, the hospital does not administer AIDS drugs like AZT to Devon, for the attitude of the staff is that he will die soon anyway, so why waste the resources. As a successful writer based in the United States, Kincaid can (and does) procure AZT for her brother, and the hospital staff is amazed when Devon begins to gain weight and recover his strength.

From this point of view, *My Brother* is similar to *A Small Place,* for both texts highlight global inequities and protest against the obscenity of poverty in a wealthy world. Kincaid rages against the distinctions between the rich and poor, distinctions that allow young people to be struck down by disease and swept away into wretched holes where they are left to die. The text thus often broadens beyond the personal narrative of Kincaid and her brother to more social issues such as economic disparities, access to medicine, and homophobia.

But Kincaid also expresses her rage at the way Antiguans scorn AIDS as a mark of shame. And there is much for her to be angry about. After all, if it had not been for her middle-class life in the United States, then Devon would have died three years earlier. Her money and her access to three years' worth of AZT prolongs his life and enables him to leave the hospital and return home. "There was no AZT on the island," Kincaid writes, "it was too expensive to be stocked, most people suffering from the disease are poor or young, not too far from being children; in a society like the one I come from, being a child is one of the definitions of vulnerability and powerlessness" (32). Here Kincaid's rage turns into cool and rational comments about the economic and political issues surrounding AIDS. Those suffering from the disease are caught up in a cycle of poverty and powerlessness that marginalizes them from the medication that can keep them alive. The implication is that free access to a drug that saves lives should be a human right. But instead pharmaceutical companies reap huge profits from the high costs of AZT and other AIDS-related drugs while simultaneously fighting the production of cheaper generic drugs that would be more accessible for the poor.

Although Kincaid is unable to change the negative attitudes that many Antiguans have toward AIDS, she finds some cause for hope in Dr. Ramsey. He has taken up AIDS as a medical, political, and educational issue, and he leads the fight against AIDS on the island. "He was kind," Kincaid writes of Ramsey, "he was loving toward people who needed him, people who were less powerful than he; he was respectful. . . . He was a very loving man and . . . wherever he went, people, ordinary people, would go out of their way to greet him" (36). Kincaid is astonished to find such a doctor in Antigua, and he becomes a symbol of hope for the future because, not only is he loving and kind, but he also runs an AIDS support group and he is devoted to educating people about safe-sex practices. In so doing he also tries to combat the shame surrounding the illness and provide Antiguans with access to the drugs that will keep them alive.

The second section of the book begins with death: the first sentence is, "My brother died" (87). And yet the simplicity of this statement does not reflect the complexity of the emotional impact that Devon's death has on Kincaid. She is profoundly affected by his death, and she relives it over and over again in her mind, analyzing it from many different perspectives. This repetition is a way to come to terms with the various stages and confusions of grief. "When the moment came, the moment I knew he was no longer alive," Kincaid writes, "I didn't know what to think, I didn't know what to feel" (87). Writing this memoir, then, becomes a way for her to sort out what she thinks and what she feels. This accounts for the circularity of the narrative, for the text keeps circling back onto itself as it moves from a contemplation of Devon's life to a meditation on his death. For instance, after stating that her brother died, Kincaid returns to the last time she saw him alive. She thus gives an account of how she saw him, two months before his death, lying in a bed and suffering from emaciation, his body left small and weak. This memory then sparks the recollection of the moment that she learns Devon has died. In this temporal movement Kincaid describes how she returned home from a trip to Miami to find her children sleeping and her husband waiting for her with the news of Devon's death. Her response is to feel relief because this pain is hers, not her husband's.

But her pain causes her to circle back to the memory of leaving her brother for the last time. She then remembers that she did not kiss him goodbye because she was angry with him: "My anger was everything to me, and in my anger lay many things, mostly made up of feelings I could not understand" (63). In this passage the reader once again becomes aware that this memoir is about fully understanding her situation. That is, the writing of the text is a way for the author to sort out her confusion and come to terms with her complex emotions in the face of death. The act of writing is, in short, also the act of working through the confusion that arises out of grief, loss, and conflicting feelings. For instance, while composing the narrative Kincaid comes to realize the source of her anger at her brother. Her anger is fueled not only by his irresponsible acts, but also by the general strain on the family, as well as the conditions under which AIDS is treated in Antigua.

The circling of the narrative continues through the second section. Kincaid's contemplation of anger leads her to think about the rage that she continues to harbor toward her mother. As if she is searching for the source of this anger, Kincaid recalls an event that happened when she was fifteen. On this occasion, while babysitting Devon, she became so involved in her books that she forgot to change her brother's diaper. When her mother returned, she was so enraged by the sight of Devon's dirty diaper (and her daughter's irresponsible behavior) that she burned all of Kincaid's books. The burning of her prized possessions causes Kincaid to direct her anger and resentment toward her mother. But her mother's irrational behavior, the author thinks, is not only reserved for her; Mrs. Drew has similar outbursts with her sons, causing them to hate her as much as Kincaid does. Kincaid then recounts the story of how her mother threw stones at Joe (the oldest of Kincaid's three brothers) for a minor transgression he had committed. In response, Joe pushed his mother to the ground, seriously injuring her. Likewise, Dalma Drew (Kincaid's middle brother) describes his mother as "evil" (54). And although he lives with her, he refuses to eat anything she cooks, referring to her only as "Mrs. Drew," not "mother." In the end, the anger that Mrs. Drew directs toward her children returns to its source. Her rage does not only hurt others; it also comes back to hurt her.

After Devon's death, the narrative of *My Brother* becomes much more fragmented and disjointed, but the form continues to reflect the content as the irrational and confused state of Kincaid's grief is mirrored in the ruptures that take place throughout the narrative. One thought shifts quickly to another thought, and the connections between the thoughts are not always apparent. For instance, before Kincaid recounts the story of Devon's funeral, she writes of the death of a four-year-old boy whose mother vomits thin liquid at the horror of burying her child. In another passage, instead of addressing Devon's bisexuality in a direct manner, Kincaid tells the tale of Freeston, a gay man who comes out of the closet and speaks of his battle with HIV only to be condemned by others. The juxtapositions of these passages capture the flow of the author's mind—a mind that has been affected by loss and mourning.

It is only toward the end of the text that Kincaid describes her brother's funeral. The minister's sermon, she thinks, is inappropriate, for he does not focus on Devon's life. Instead he speaks of how the family will one day be reunited in heaven; Kincaid responds to this by thinking that she would really prefer not to see her family again. Healing comes, for her, not in the thought of seeing her brother again, but in writing about him. For writing about his death enables her to understand Devon's life, death, and her own emotional responses toward him. This point is more generally underscored in the conclusion when Kincaid once again connects writing to death by invoking the memory of William Shawn. "Almost all of my life as a writer," she states, "everything I wrote I expected Mr. Shawn to read, and so when I first heard of my brother dying and immediately knew I would write about him, I thought of Mr. Shawn, but Mr. Shawn had just died, too" (197). Here Kincaid identifies Shawn as the "perfect reader"; the person she will always write for. And even Shawn's death does not put an end to this, for Kincaid continues to see him as her main audience. The act of writing, then, keeps the memory of William Shawn alive, just as Kincaid's composition of this memoir combines memory and writing to create a memorial of her brother. But this memorial does not simply commemorate a person who has died. Rather it is more for the living than the dead, as it helps Kincaid to understand the complexities of grief, mourning, and loss.

Overall, the writing style employed in *My Brother* brings together the language used by the characters with the themes that are developed in the narration. This is important for understanding the diction, point of view, and symbolism of the text. For instance, family members each speak with a distinct diction, and their language contributes to an understanding of their characterization. The language used by Kincaid is formal and distant. In fact, her economic and precise sentences are juxtaposed to the more informal diction used by her mother and brothers. Devon in particular says things like, "Me mek wutlessness ah me life, man" (I have made worthlessness of my life) and "Me carn belieb me had dis chupidness" (I cannot belief that I have this stupidness); the "stupidness" is what he calls HIV and AIDS (29). This oral use of language is significant because Kincaid tells us that she cannot always understand what her brother is saying. Indeed her alienation from Antiguan English becomes apparent when Dr. Ramsey is speaking to Devon about being HIV positive. "I could not understand what they were saying," she writes, "they spoke so fast, it was the most animated I had seen my brother since I first saw him lying there dying. He even laughed out loud at something Dr. Ramsey said, something I did not understand" (33). This lack of comprehension reflects the distance that separates Kincaid from both her family and her native land. She is an outsider in her own family and a foreigner in her homeland. Devon even finds Kincaid's way of speaking to be comical. He makes fun of her strange accent and her bizarre expressions. From his perspective, his sister speaks in a foreign tongue, even when she is "at home."

In her review of *My Brother*, Anna Quindlen describes Kincaid's writing style as follows: "The stylistic ground she covers in this book is also recognizable from her past work, the endless incantatory sentences a contrast to the simple words and images—a tower built of small bricks."[15] This mix of spellbinding sentences with straightforward diction is consistent with the frank and startling honesty with which Kincaid reveals herself and her family. The narrative is, among other things, a search for truth, but there is always the indication that truth will remain absent. This leads to the narrative repetition of self-evident facts: everyone will experience loss in one way or another, and death will always eventually overcome life (88). By repeating things that can be taken for granted, the author is not only dealing with her own sense of loss, but she is also making the point that there are very few givens in life and that everything must be repeatedly examined in order to determine what is true and what is false.

And yet even those things that we take to be true are also questioned throughout the text. For instance, after Kincaid states that everyone dies, she goes on to complicate her statement by saying, "The dead never die, and I now say this—the dead never die—as if it were new, as if no one had ever noticed this before.

. . . The dead never die, let me just say it again" (121–22). This passage is typical of the writing style that Kincaid develops in *My Brother,* for it does two things: it adds complexity to an earlier section of the text while it also engages in the act of repetition. The statement "the dead never die" is repeated three times in the space of a few lines. Such repetition expresses the state of confusion that accompanies grief. That is, by repeating things the author acknowledges that she is on unstable ground and that she does not know exactly where she stands. Moreover, the repetitions combine with the multilayered meanings of the statements to convey a sense of ambivalence. In another passage, for instance, Kincaid writes, "My talk was full of pain, it was full of misery, it was full of anger, there was no peace in it, there was much sorrow, but there was no peace to it" (181). Here words and ideas are repeated. And this pattern is significant in that it conveys a sense of ambivalence through contradiction, for the sentence is in juxtaposition with earlier sentences telling us that Kincaid derives peace and healing from writing about Devon's illness.

Death, then, is connected to life, and life is connected to motherhood. Indeed mothering is an important theme in the text, a theme that is tied to birth and the source of life but that is also linked to death and destruction. Kincaid says that the extraordinary thing about her mother's love for her children is her ability "to turn [it] into a weapon for their destruction" (61). But this sharp condemnation is tempered by Kincaid's praise of her mother's capacity for maternal devotion: she describes her mother's tireless nursing of Devon as he lies in the hospital, and Kincaid recalls the great tenderness and devotion that her mother expressed when she fell ill as a child. As a maternal figure, then, Mrs. Drew is described as loving and kind to her young children and to Devon when he is in the childlike state of illness. However, this love and nurturing turns to hate and destruction when "her children are trying to be grown-up people—adults" (17). When Kincaid is struggling to become a writer in New York, for example, her mother's words are harsh and destructive: "It serves you right, you are always trying to do things you know you can't do" (17). Such cruelty speaks to the complicated portrait that Kincaid paints of her mother. On the one hand, Mrs. Drew is a giver of life, someone who is nurturing and compassionate; on the other hand, she seeks to rob her adult children of life by undermining their confidence, taking away their independence, and destroying their ambitions.

Kincaid then considers her own role as a mother. She reflects upon the fact that mothers are often loved and hated by their children. From time to time, she writes, a mother will produce negative feelings in her child. And as she thinks about her own relationship to her son, she concludes that these contradictory feelings are a normal aspect of the mother-child dynamic. "This state of profound contradiction," she says of her son's relationship to her, "loving me and hating me, is what will be for the rest of his life, if I am a good mother to him. This is the best that I can be. If I should fail him . . . he will experience something everlastingly bitter and awful: I know this, the taste of this awfulness, this bitterness, is in my mouth every day" (62).

But Kincaid also indicates that she and her mother share a common love, for they both have a great passion for gardening. Here motherhood is connected to nurturing, and nurturing is linked to gardening. Indeed in a 2002 interview Kincaid was asked where her love of gardening came from. "I'm sure it's directly related to my mother," she answered, "She was a gardener. She has an amazing green thumb and her power over her plants is absolute. She grows things that other people can't even grow, but she grows tired of them and just throws them away. I always admired her ability to grow things."[16] With this answer, Kincaid captures one of the paradoxes of her mother. She has a great ability to nurture things (she devotes herself to helping things grow), but this is combined with a cold distance (she tires of the things once they are grown, and then she rejects them).

But gardening is, in *My Brother,* also used as a more general metaphor for nurturing. For instance, when Kincaid writes about Freeston, the AIDS educator and activist, she describes the wonderful garden that she finds at his home. This lush and beautiful plant life is symbolic of the harmony of his family life: "He lived with [his mother] in a house with a beautiful garden full of zinnias and cosmos and some impatiens and all sorts of shrubs and with glossy and variegated leaves" (147). This image of healthy foliage is contrasted with the plant imagery that Kincaid uses to describe Devon's life: "In his life there had been no flowering, his life was the opposite of that, a flowering, his life was like the bud that sets but, instead of opening into a flower, turns brown and falls off at your feet" (148).

This symbolism is significant in terms of Kincaid's development as a writer—the symbolic potential of gardening is a subject that she explores in her later work. Although Kincaid began writing about gardens some years ago in her columns for the *New Yorker,* her most recent book-length projects have focused almost exclusively on gardening. In her early garden writing, the garden was often a point of departure for reflections about personal, cultural, and historical issues. But in her more recent books, gardening is thoroughly explored as a metaphoric device. Kincaid discusses this in her essay "In History," wherein she links Columbus's colonizing project of renaming the new world with Linnaeus's renaming of the plants that the merchant George Clifford accumulated during his travels for the Dutch East India Company.[17] Likewise, in *My Garden (Book)* (1999), Kincaid joins together colonial history with her own gardening experience to consider the implications of how the English idea of the garden affected conceptions of space in the British empire.[18] In this work Kincaid extends far beyond the musings found in her early garden writing, using the garden to ponder the history of slavery, the privilege of wealth, and the arrogance of the ruling classes. As in all of Kincaid's work, these texts blend together autobiography with colonial history, and gardening lore is linked to passages about her own gardening techniques to illustrate the symbolic potential of the garden metaphor.[19]

Sexuality is another central theme in *My Brother*. And throughout the text Kincaid engages with a paradox at the heart of sexuality: the act of sex can give life, but it also has the power to take life away. Sexual activity, that is, gives life to Devon, but that same activity kills him. Moreover, the fact that Devon continues to engage in unprotected sex once he has been diagnosed with HIV makes him a carrier of death: his acts and his silence are a potentially deathly combination. From this perspective, sexuality is linked to power, and this is significant because Devon can only express himself through his sexuality. Even when he is frail and dying in the hospital, he expresses his attraction to a young woman: "While staring pointedly at her crotch," Kincaid recounts, "he said some words to her, letting her know that he would like to have sex with her" (43). For Devon, self-expression does not arise out of speaking or writing but through his sexuality. This point is highlighted when Kincaid describes Devon's second (and final) stay in the hospital. When she entered his hospital room, Kincaid recalls, Devon expressed his suffering by exposing himself to her. "He suddenly," she writes, "tore his pyjama bottoms away from his waist, revealing his penis, and he grabbed his penis in his hand and held it up . . . it was covered with sores and on the sores was a white substance, almost creamy, almost floury, a fungus" (91). In this scene Devon does not speak, but instead he reveals his pain by gesturing toward his infected penis. The silence of this passage is significant, for the organ that he has always used to express himself is no longer functional. At this stage of his illness, he has lost his only means of expression.

Kincaid thus treats sexuality as a highly complex issue. Sexual identity and sexual acts are represented as having serious implications for relations of power, marginalization, and self-definition. As a result, Kincaid is frank about her own interest in sex: "On the whole," she states, "I like to know whom people have sex with, and a description of it I find especially interesting. My own life, from a sexual standpoint, can be described as a monument to boring conventionality. And so perhaps because of this I have a great interest in other people's personal lives" (41). However, for all of her interest in sex, she is unable to discover the facts surrounding Devon's sexual history. It is only after Devon's death that Kincaid finds out that he sometimes had sex with other men.

In fact, the gaps in Kincaid's knowledge are filled in by a chance meeting with a near stranger. When Kincaid is giving a reading at a bookstore in Chicago, she meets a woman from Antigua whom she met three years earlier at an AIDS support group organized by Dr. Ramsey. This woman, whom Kincaid refers to as a white lesbian, knows that Devon is dead. She offers her condolences to Kincaid and then speaks of the scorn and derision heaped upon homosexual men in Antigua. She tells Kincaid about how she used to invite gay men to her home on Sundays so that they could meet each other in a relaxed atmosphere. Devon, she says, often visited her on these occasions (165).

Kincaid is surprised to hear this. She did not know about her brother's sexual identity, and when faced with the news, she experiences a sense of estrangement and dislocation. Indeed this estrangement is at the heart of the memoir, for Kincaid uses it to emphasize the unknowability of those people who surround us. Even those people we love, she suggests, are strangers to us. But instead of feeling anger, bitterness, or sadness at her brother's concealment, she feels a new empathy with her brother: "Who he really was—not a single sense of identity but all the complexities of who he was—he could not express fully: his fear of being laughed at, his fear of meeting with the scorn of the people he knew best were overwhelming and he could not live with all of it openly" (169). This touching image of his sensitivity and anxieties is followed by Kincaid's comment that he could never be himself (he could never express who he was) because of the attitudes of the people around him. She recognizes, then, that she too could not have expressed herself or developed a whole sense of self had she stayed in Antigua. "His homosexuality is one thing," she states, "and my becoming a writer is another altogether, but this truth is not lost to me: I could not have become a writer while living among the people I knew best, I could not have become myself while living among the people I knew best . . . in his life there had been no flowering" (169).

This identification with Devon does not lead to an appropriation of his voice because she recognizes the specificities of their distinct situations and lives. However, Kincaid does seek—as she does in A Small Place—to make connections between people, and her connection to her brother runs deep. During his funeral, for example, she is overcome with a sense of loss as she mourns the fact the she will never hear his voice again. This loss and the deep connection she feels toward him has, she implies, inspired her to explore his life in the form of this memoir. But in the end *My Brother* asks if we can ever really know another person. Perhaps all we can do, Kincaid suggests, is get to know ourselves.

CHAPTER 5

Recent Novels

The Autobiography of My Mother and Mr. Potter

The Autobiography of My Mother

Jamaica Kincaid's novel *The Autobiography of My Mother* was published in 1996. The main protagonist of this book is Xuela Claudette Richardson, the daughter of a Carib mother and a half-Scots, half-African father. Xuela's mother, though, dies giving birth to Xuela, and as a result she grows up motherless in the care of her father's laundress. The narrative is told in the first-person voice of Xuela: she recounts the story of her childhood perceptions, her experience of being seduced as a schoolgirl, her passionate affair with a stevedore, and her marriage to an English doctor. At the center of these events is Xuela's continual search for knowledge about the history of her mother. In fact, this search develops into a kind of obsession wherein Xuela tries to compose a portrait of her mother—a woman whom Xuela has neither seen nor spoken to. Thus her imagination takes over, and she conjures up images of her mother's feelings and passions. She imagines the first time that her mother met her father and the way in which their relationship grew into love. She also constructs a narrative in which her mother is part of a dying race—the race of the Carib people, whose culture and language is facing extinction. However, Xuela's search for her mother is also a search for herself, for this "autobiography" is a way for her to find out who she is, where she comes from, and where she is going.

The Autobiography of My Mother was nominated for the 1997 National Book Critics Circle Award for fiction. Reviews of the novel were generally positive, although some reviewers stated that the narrative did not offer much hope or optimism for the future. Margaria Fichtner, for example, wrote that Kincaid's powerful themes and visual writing style produced heartbreak in the reader: "From first page to last, Kincaid relates Xuela's remarkable story with a richness and lyricism that can be almost heartbreaking. Some passages read like word pictures; others read like psalms."[1] Likewise, another reviewer, Paul Grondahl, foregrounds the bleakness of the narrative by calling attention to the "grim and painful life on the Caribbean island of Dominica." For Grondahl, Xuela's story is a "shocking, cruel tale" of "the tyranny of the past and attempts to escape it."[2] What many of these critics overlook, though, is the complexity of the narrative form. The novel unfolds as a 228-page monologue rendered in unconventional, haunting prose. The text is devoid of direct speech, and there is not a single quotation or line of dialogue. Instead the reader hears the incantatory voice of the seventy-year-old Xuela, who looks back on her life and narrates her hardships with verve and emotion.

Some reviewers found the title of Kincaid's novel to be puzzling. Paul Grondahl, for instance, states that the title is mysterious because "Xuela's mother dies in childbirth," and he suggests that this is the "least autobiographical" of Kincaid's novels.[3] But such a comment misses the title's playful echoing of important modernist works such as James Weldon Johnson's *Autobiography of an Ex-Colored Man* (1912) and Gertrude Stein's *Autobiography of Alice B. Toklas* (1933). Indeed Kincaid's debt to modernism highlights the multilayered and self-reflexive nature of the text while at the same time building upon the experimental style cultivated by her modernist predecessors. Moreover, Kincaid borrows the title (and the mother-daughter theme) from Rosellen Brown's 1976 novel, *The Autobiography of My Mother.* Brown's version is set in New York City in the 1970s and explores the relationship between Gerda Stein and her daughter Renata. The two characters are locked in a consuming and painful battle, and yet they are unable to distance themselves from one another. Gerda comes to realize that her life and her daughter's are bound together in deep, significant ways. In fact, the bond is so deep that Gerda even states that they "were to share one life" between them.[4] Kincaid's 1996 Caribbean version is hauntingly reminiscent of Brown's text, for Xuela's life is intimately bound to the life and death of her mother.

It is important to note that Kincaid's *The Autobiography of My Mother* does not conform to the traditional generic conventions of the autobiography by presenting a writer who is also a narrator, a character, and a historical figure. Rather the text focuses on a fictional character who speaks in a first-person monologue, relaying the verbal communication between the characters. This means that the voices of the characters are mediated through Xuela's point of view and that the reader is presented with Xuela's perspective on the world around her. And yet Xuela's monopoly on voice (and the subsequent expression of her worldview) does not suppress other perspectives, for she is not outside of the social discourses that surround her, and thus her individuality is developed in relation to her social interaction with others. Her voice, then, is not singular or monolithic; instead it is a mixture of her own speech and the external discourses that influence her.

As a character, Xuela is a product of Kincaid's imagination. However, she also moves between the imaginary world of the text and the real world of Kincaid's life. After all, Kincaid's books always combine fact and fiction, and this novel is no exception. In a recent interview, for instance, Kincaid stated that the story of Xuela "is autobiographical in ideas but not in situation."[5] And she explains this statement by noting that the text takes elements from her mother's and grandmother's lives and weaves them together to create an imaginative story of her own maternal family history. Xuela, then, can be read as a depiction of Kincaid's fictional mother, and this relates directly to the complexity of the title. That is, the word "autobiography" might be read as being spoken by Kincaid, who bases much of Xuela's story on the life of her own real mother. But the same word might also be understood as spoken by the fictional character Xuela, whose life as an orphan inspires her to recover the story of her own dead mother.

Kincaid's comments in interviews can help shed light on the complexity of this novel as her personal voice (the one that speaks outside of her fiction) is often enlightening in that it clarifies her literary project. For example, in a 1994 interview Kincaid said that her writing "has been very autobiographical" and the events in her texts are "true for her, if not for other people."[6] This slippage between the realm of fiction and the world of autobiography is sophisticated because Kincaid's work is never solely personal or individual. For her narrators, including Xuela, are never cut off from the communities that surround them. On the contrary, the individual—the "I" narrator of the work—is always intimately connected to, and influenced by, the public sphere. In this particular text, Xuela is linked to a community that influences her perceptions of the world. This is important because, for Kincaid, communities are products of histories, and the history of a specific place has a profound impact upon the individual. If, for instance, a community is marked by a history of colonization and subjugation, then individuality will be formed in relation to that past. Thus the text illustrates how individuality is not only personal; it is also developed out of historical narratives and relationships with others.[7]

Kincaid dedicates *The Autobiography of My Mother* to the Nobel Prize–winning poet and fellow West Indies native, Derek Walcott. This is not surprising when we consider that Walcott has been a longtime admirer and supporter of Kincaid's literary project. "As she writes a sentence," Walcott says of Kincaid, "the temperature of it psychologically is that it heads toward its own contradiction. It's as if the sentence is discovering itself, discovering how it feels. And that is astonishing, because it's one thing to be able to write a good declarative sentence; it's another thing to catch the temperature of the narrator, the narrator's feeling. And that's universal, and not provincial in any way."[8] In comments such as this, Walcott identifies Kincaid as an international author, not a regional Caribbean writer. He asserts that her writing is unique in both style and form, suggesting that her content must be read as universal rather than personal. But Walcott's lavish praise is not the only reason why Kincaid dedicated this novel to him. There is a thematic connection between this novel and Walcott's writing about mixed cultural heritage. For instance, in his poem "Far Cry from Africa," the speaker states, "I who am poisoned with the blood of both, / Where shall I turn, divided to the vein?"[9] These lines are akin to Kincaid's characterization of Xuela, who is portrayed through her mixed bloodlines and cultural hybridity. Part Carib, part African, and part Scots, Xuela has a fragmented identity and is torn between various races, communities, and histories. Where should she turn? With whom should she identify? And where does she belong?

Xuela is never able fully to answer these questions. As a result, the novel begins and ends with the realization that she is ultimately alone, even though she carries with her voices from the past—voices that demand expression.

Contradictions, as Walcott notes, are quite common in Kincaid's writing. And Kincaid would agree: "To me," she says, "the truth is that things mean many things at once, and all of them opposed to each other, and all of them true."[10] This is significant, for *The Autobiography of My Mother* appears to make contradictory statements through its seemingly self-divided rhetoric. The novel juxtaposes images and symbols in order to represent Xuela's divided self. But the juxtapositions also highlight the contradictory omens that Kincaid articulates in her shifting moves from nonfiction to fiction. In fact, throughout the novel Kincaid transforms the rigid contradictions in her nonfiction into the images, symbols, and ideas for her powerful fiction.

One such transformation is, of course, the conflicted (and contradictory) relationship to the maternal figure. "My mother died the moment I was born," Xuela states, "and so for my whole life there was nothing standing between myself and eternity; at my back was always a bleak, black wind."[11] This first sentence of the novel is striking for its juxtapositions: the giving of life is also the taking of life, and the beginning of one narrative marks the end of another. Moreover, Xuela's response to this loss is filled with tensions and conflicting emotions. On the one hand, she expresses a sense of liberation and freedom, for, as she says, there is now nothing standing between herself and eternity. Her life is, in other words, to be determined by her, not by the influence of a stifling maternal figure. On the other hand, she expresses pain at the fact that she will never know her maternal lineage, aware that knowledge of the past contributes to identity formation in the present. But because of the absent mother, Xuela can never fully know her history, and thus she experiences a void that is articulated in the "bleak, black wind" that is always at her back.

After the death of her mother, Xuela's father abandons her. He places her in the care of Ma Eunice, a poor woman who washes clothes to support herself and her children. Xuela, then, becomes lost in an imagined conception of her dead mother, and she struggles to find a voice in order to transcend the silenced fate that has enveloped her. With neither father nor mother, the narrator is forced to discover herself outside of any parental direction, and she must find a place for herself in the community of Dominica. Her father comes to see her once a fortnight (when he collects his laundry), but his appearance is sporadic. On one occasion when he fails to appear, Xuela turns to Ma Eunice and asks "Where is my father?" (7). Her voice, she is surprised to find, utters these words in the English language. This is surprising because Creole is the language spoken around her; in fact, Xuela has never heard English spoken, and yet she speaks these words. In this unreal moment, Xuela speaks in a language that is not her own—a language she has never even heard. This implies that Xuela lacks a mother tongue, and thus she must work hard to discover a voice with which she can express herself to others.

Furthermore, Xuela's English utterance raises issues about the history of colonization on the island of Dominica. For Xuela's lost mother tongue symbolizes the history of imperialism that includes the eradication of Native languages and, in turn, the destruction of a Carib cultural identity. As Xuela goes on to say, "That the first words I said were in a language of a people I would never like or love is not now a mystery to me; everything in my life, good or bad, to which I am inextricably bound is a source of pain" (7).

From an early age, then, Xuela is aware of the power structures that surround her. She understands how power is tied to language and historical events. At school, for instance, Xuela recognizes that the other students identify her in a specific way based on the history of Dominica. "I was of the African people, but not exclusively," she states, "My mother was a Carib woman, and when they looked at me this is what they saw: The Carib people had been defeated and then exterminated . . . the African people had been defeated but survived. When they looked at me, they saw the Carib people" (16). Xuela, in short, has the mark of the vanquished thrust upon her by the community. Her fellow students cast her in the mold of a people who have largely died out, a culture that has been eradicated. They see her as a lost ancestor of the Carib people—people who settled in the Caribbean and the Lesser Antilles after migrating there from the Orinoco rainforests of Venezuela. The students in her class therefore regard her as an ancestor of those who were defeated, displaced, and largely eradicated after the arrival of Columbus in 1492.[12]

In this context, the death of Xuela's Carib mother and the loss of her language both speak to the European eradication of Dominica's Native culture. Indeed, by characterizing Xuela as an orphan, Kincaid dramatizes the history of the island through the isolation of the individual, for Xuela's dead Carib mother symbolizes her own alienation as a Caribbean subject. Thus her childhood socialization must occur outside of a familial or Carib sphere of influence. She must, in essence, go through a process of self-fashioning. But during her individuation, Xuela refuses to let go of her mother's life, and she composes a fantastic narrative wherein her own identity is formed in relation to her mother. However, because Xuela's only contact with her mother was the birth-death event that began the narrative, Xuela inherits a Carib history of loss, and she, in turn, carries on a past that is marked by violence and death.

From this perspective, Kincaid's story of the dead Carib mother and a part-Carib daughter is an exploration of the silenced history of a people who have been lost. Yet *The Autobiography of My Mother* also recognizes the impossibility of piecing together and voicing this silenced history. What is lost cannot be regained, and this recognition sparks a series of questions throughout the text: What is Xuela's connection to a past that cannot be recaptured? Can she speak for her mother, or the Carib people in general? And can Xuela ever compose the autobiography of a mother whom she has never known? These questions are invoked but never answered. Instead Xuela speaks of her own life in relation to a life she has not lived: her mother's. And this leads to a central paradox in Xuela's story, for her mother will always be part of her, but at the same time her mother will always be unavailable. This situation defines Xuela's life, and it compels her to compose this "autobiography."

But this obsession with the mother-daughter bond is not only personal. For Kincaid uses this bond once again to address larger themes, including political issues such as colonization and marginalization. Kincaid explains this in a 1992 interview: "There are wider implications for the mother and daughter relationship. . . . I'm really writing about mother country and subject daughter country. It certainly led me to see that I was obsessed with the powerful and the powerless. . . . I've outgrown the domestic implications of the mother and the daughter, and it now has wider implications for me."[13] In *The Autobiography of My*

Mother these wider implications arise out of the relationship between power and the mother country. Because Xuela is a part-Carib woman and defined as one of the vanquished people, her country (Dominica) is, like her mother, lost to her. Due to the history of war and violence, Xuela is born into a place that is not her mother country at all. Rather it is ruled by someone else, by another group of people to which she does not belong. Xuela's abandonment by her mother, then, mirrors the abandoned nation of Dominica—a place that was infantilized by a European mother country and then left orphaned after it struggled to gain independence.

This loss is painful, and Xuela expresses the pain of abandonment in a letter she writes to her father. In this letter she "utters the plaintive cry of a small wounded animal," and she begs him to rescue her from her state of alienation and isolation (19). Xuela would really like to address this letter to her mother (the "person of whom I could see only her heels"), but because her mother is dead she turns to her only living parent. She writes, "My dear Papa, you are the only person I have left in the world, no one loves me, only you can, I am beaten with words, I am beaten with sticks, I am beaten with stones . . . only you can save me" (19). Here Xuela expresses her personal despair—a despair that her father does not respond to. But her experience also replicates the violence and oppression suffered by the Carib people. She is beaten because of her heritage; she is struck down because she comes from a vanquished society; and she is oppressed because she has neither a mother nor a mother country. Xuela, then, is defined not by her parents, but by the history that she inherits through her matrilineal line.

Her father eventually responds to her pleas. He removes her from her harsh environment and takes her to live in his new home. But this does not alleviate Xuela's pain, for her father has married a (nameless) woman who is overwhelmed by jealousy. This woman despises Xuela; in fact, she wants to see her husband's child dead: "I felt as each minute passed," Xuela states, "that someone wanted me dead" (30). And indeed her stepmother attempts to use obeah magic on Xuela, giving her a "poisonous" necklace intended to kill her. But Xuela refuses to wear the necklace, choosing instead to put it around the neck of her stepmother's dog. Within twenty-four hours, the dog goes mad and dies (34).

Xuela's tense relationship with this woman leads back to the theme of the mother tongue: her stepmother refuses to speak to her in English. Instead she will only talk to Xuela in what is considered to be the degraded dialect of French patois: "She spoke to me then in French patois. . . . She would do this to me through all the time we knew each other . . . [and] I recognized this to be an attempt on her part to make an illegitimate of me, to associate me with the made-up language of the people regarded as not real—the shadow people, the forever humiliated, the forever low" (30). Her father's wife thus uses language as an assertion of superiority; her speech is an attempt to marginalize Xuela, an act that is consistent with her attempt to kill Xuela using obeah practices. For her use of patois casts Xuela in the position of the socially dead, forcing her to adopt the mother tongue of the vanquished people. This excludes Xuela from any association with the living culture of the island—the African and European cultures that have survived.

At the age of fourteen, Xuela escapes her father's house. She goes to live in Roseau, the capital of Dominica, and she moves in with her father's acquaintance, Monsieur LaBatte. Xuela begins to develop a "deep friendship" with Madame LaBatte, and as their friendship grows, the older woman gives Xuela one of the dresses that she used to wear as a youth. This offer is significant: it signals an intimacy between the two women, but, more important, it marks Madame LaBatte's desire to turn back the clock, to be "the person she used to be when she first wore the dress" (68). Madame LaBatte, then, seeks to relive her youth through Xuela, for she has a deep-seated desire to go back and recapture "the things she had wanted, the things she had not received" (68). Madame LaBatte has always wanted a child, wanted to become a mother, but she has never been able to bear children. As a result, her desire to return to her youth through Xuela is also connected to her frustrated longing to conceive a child. She thus decides to give her husband to Xuela (to "make a gift . . . of her husband") in the hope that the younger woman will become pregnant. As Xuela states, Madame LaBatte "wanted a child, had wanted a child . . . and she wanted a child I might have" (77).

Xuela decides to sleep with Monsieur LaBatte, so he takes her to "the room in which he count[s] his money," undresses her, and has sex with her (70). Xuela's emotional response is a mixture of pain, pleasure, and sadness. The pleasure of their physical contact is diminished by his desire to possess her as he possesses the money that surrounds him. In fact, the room is filled with "many coins, their sides turned heads up . . . [displaying] the face of the king" (71). During their lovemaking, Xuela becomes distracted by this iconography; she gazes around the room and takes note of all of the coins "lined up" on the shelves. The symbolism of this scene is quite striking. Monsieur LaBatte wants to acquire Xuela as he acquires wealth, for he can only associate love with money and capital. Moreover, Xuela suggests that he identifies himself through his coins, displaying the figure of the king as a way of linking himself to a symbol of power. Indeed the king, who figures as the ultimate image of the patriarch, casts his gaze over Xuela as she lies under LaBatte. Such an identification suggests that LaBatte sees himself as the patriarch (and king) of this place, and his penetration of Xuela is an exertion of his power as well as a manifestation of his desire to conceive an heir who will inherit his estate.

Power, though, is fluid rather than fixed. And when Xuela becomes pregnant with LaBatte's child, she decides to abort it. This decision is an act of empowerment; it is an assertion of identity that refuses to allow Madame and Monsieur LaBatte to determine her life. But it is also more than this: when she is told that she is "with child," Xuela feels that she "will die" and that she is "standing in a black hole" (82). Motherhood, then, is associated with death and the erasure of the self. As a result, Xuela rejects the pattern of birth and death that she experienced with her own mother; she terminates the pregnancy by visiting "Sange-Sange" and drinking a cup of "thick black syrup" that causes her body to feel like a "volcano of pain" for four days (82). During this time she lies in a small hole on Sange-Sange's dirt floor, and when the pain ceases, the fetus has been aborted. This death—the termination of her pregnancy—has a positive impact on Xuela, and she feels as if she has been born again: "I was a new person then, I knew things I had not known before, I knew things that you can know only if you have been through what I had just been through" (83). Here the abortion is not defined in terms of death or destruction. Rather the experience offers Xuela a rebirth through self-knowledge and the development of individuality. The abortion is, in short, an act that arises out of her conscious choice to save her own life instead of giving it over to the birth of a child: "I carried my own life," she states, "in my own hands" (83).

Xuela thus gains a sense of self by rejecting motherhood. In fact, after her abortion, she states that she will "never become a mother"; she will never conceive a child again (97). Xuela is happy with this situation, and the pleasure that she gains from this knowledge is a conscious rebellion against the socially subscribed role of mother. She thus embraces her independence and claims her body for herself. This claim is furthered in her celebration of autoeroticism: "My hands traveled up and down all over my own body in a loving caress, finally coming to the soft, moist spot between my legs, and a gasp of pleasure had escaped my lips which I would allow no one to hear" (43). Xuela savors this private act of sexual independence, and masturbation is a way for her to maintain a position of sexual control by refusing the reproduction and regeneration of the familial line. In fact, Xuela celebrates the act of touching herself, and she relishes the pleasures that she finds in her body. Even during her sexual affairs with men, she describes touching her body to arouse her (and her partner's) pleasure: "The scene of me placing my hand between my legs and then enjoying the smell of myself and [him] watching me lasted until the usual sudden falling of dark, and so when he came closer to me and asked me to remove my clothes, I said, quite sure of myself, knowing that I was wanted, that it was too dark, I could not see" (70).

In this passage, Xuela uses her sexuality as a form of power. She is in control, for she not only arouses herself and her partner, but she also refuses to remove her clothes because it is too dark. Here she takes on the desiring gaze of the male eye, for she wants to see him in the sexual act. She thus refuses to remain passive; instead she returns the desiring gaze that is usually ascribed to male sexuality. Such an act combines with the celebration of her bodily smell to reject any source of shame that might be tied to her body or to her desire. In a recent interview,

Kincaid explains these aspects of Xuela's characterization by stating that "a woman's sexuality—a woman's body—is also a weapon against her. This thing that is most natural . . . is this incredible source of shame. All the things about men seem to be a source of inspiration and pride, but a woman is constantly hearing the opposite. . . . It's always one thing or another with your body. . . . But I've decided that everything that is a source of shame you should just wear brazenly."[14]

Xuela's sexual development continues when she meets a stevedore, Roland, and they have a passionate affair. The mere sight of Roland makes Xuela "feel hot" and "perspire" until the "water seep[s] through" her dress, revealing the outline of her breasts and nipples (165). Her body responds to Roland with intense pleasure, and she refuses to hide her passion; she longs for his sexually charged gaze and the feeling of his hands on her body. In fact, during their affair, Xuela makes a "false pocket" in her skirt that does "not have a bottom" so that Roland can place "his hand inside the pocket" and reach "all the way down to touch inside her" (177). Xuela thus puts great stock in the power of her body: the power to give herself pleasure and the power to give pleasure to others. From this perspective, she also celebrates the beauty of Roland's body and the powerful physical attraction that he inspires in her. She describes her happiness when she looks at his mouth, feels his tongue, and touches his skin. "I bathed my face then between his legs," she says, "he smelled of curry and onions, for those were the things he had been unloading all day; other times when I bathed my face between his legs—for I did it often, I liked doing it—he would smell of sugar, or flour" (169).

Roland, however, is not satisfied by the mere giving and receiving of pleasure. He wants to dominate Xuela's body by impregnating her. On one occasion, Xuela reveals that "Roland looked at me, his face expressing confusion. Why did I not bear his children? He could feel the times that I was fertile, and yet each month blood flowed away from me. . . . When I saw him like that, on his face a look that was a mixture—sorrow, dumb-foundedness, defeat—I felt sorrow for him, for his life was reduced to . . . women" (175–76). By contrast, Xuela is "over-joyed" by the sight of her menstruation each month. The blood is a sign that Roland cannot claim her body; he cannot take control of her. Roland, however, feels that he is defeated by this monthly occurrence. It strikes a blow to his manhood and weakens the very foundations of his sense of self as he can only define himself by the power that he exerts over women.

Xuela also meets an Englishman named Philip Bailey. Philip is described as the "opposite" of Roland, and Xuela does not find the Englishman to be physically attractive or sexually exciting (163). Instead she identifies Philip in negative ways, referring to him as a "white doctor" who is marked by the violence of his colonizing forefathers. "By the time Philip was born," Xuela states, "all the bad deeds had already been committed; he was an heir, generations of people had died and left him something" (146). But Philip does not only inherit this past; he also repeats it by acting out the history of conquest through his attempts to dominate nature. He is obsessed with "the growing of flowering plants for no other reason than the pleasure of it and making these plants do exactly what he wanted them to do; and it made great sense that he would be drawn to this activity, for it is an act of conquest, benign though it may be" (143). For Xuela, Philip's compulsive actions are futile and useless. She sees him as reenacting a fruitless ritual that duplicates the tragic legacy of colonial domination.

Xuela is also highly critical of Philip's wife. She describes this woman as a white person who can only gain a sense of self through the denigration of black people. In fact, Philip's wife is particularly cruel to black women, treating them as if they are slaves and animals. Xuela highlights these negative qualities by describing her in the following way: "She was a lady, I was a woman, and this distinction for her was very important; it allowed her to believe that I would not associate the ordinary, the everyday . . . with her, and a small act of cruelty was elevated to a rite of civilization" (158). Xuela introduces this woman to an intoxicant that is produced by the white flowers of a beautiful weed. Eventually Philip's wife becomes addicted to the effect of this hallucinatory drug, and she develops a compulsive and insatiable appetite for the plant. The color of this plant is symbolic, for this English lady becomes addicted to its "whiteness" and she becomes poisoned by it. In the end, her consumption of the plant's drug leads to her demise. The infusions from the flower start to darken her skin, and just before she dies her skin turns, quite ironically, completely black.

Xuela then decides to marry Philip. She makes this decision despite the fact that she sees him as a profoundly unhappy man: his privilege, wealth, and status have never made him satisfied or content. In fact, Xuela views Philip's dissatisfaction as partially responsible for their marriage; his unhappy restlessness, she states, has taken him to this "far corner of the world" and "led him into her bed" (237). From Xuela's perspective, their relationship is based on power relations, and as she begins to feel more comfortable in their marriage, she starts to exert more power over him. She thus inverts the traditional hierarchy in which the white male colonist holds the seat of power. And when the couple moves out of Roseau to a rural area of Dominica,

Philip comes to rely on Xuela more and more. His powerlessness arises out of his confusion and disorientation—two states of mind that are heightened when he and Xuela go to live in a Carib community. Here Philip becomes marginalized as an outsider, a foreigner. Yet he still attempts to reassert his power and regain his position of authority by acting out the colonizing compulsion to categorize and label all that he sees. But he is unable to gain control because "he now live[s] in a world in which he could not speak the language" (224). Indeed Philip's mother tongue has no place here; he cannot communicate with others or impose discourses on the community. Still, he refuses to admit defeat, and, as in his gardening, he attempts to dominate and control the Carib community through categorization and taxonomy. In the end, though, he is unable to master this community (a community of "vanquished" people) because he is unable to understand their language. Placed within this context, Philip figuratively dies, and Xuela exerts her power: "I mediated for him," she asserts, "I translated for him. . . . I blocked his entrance into all the worlds he had come to know" (224).

Xuela lives to be an old woman. As she waits for her own death to come, she reflects upon the fact that most of the people she has known have already died. Some of these people were strong, and others were weak; some were victimizers, and others were victimized; and some were colonizing, while still others were colonized. Death has taken them all. The powerful and the helpless all meet the same fate: nobody can avert the inevitability of death.

Mr. Potter

In 2002, Kincaid published a novel titled *Mr. Potter*. This text continues the author's earlier ruminations on family, identity, loss, and colonization. The Mr. Potter of the title is a philander-ing chauffeur from Antigua, who is described as a man who walks unquestioningly and unselfconsciously through life. He is also the father of the narrator, Elaine Potter Richardson, who shares the birth name of the author. But this book is not a biog-raphy or a history of Kincaid's father. Rather it is a piece of fic-tion in which the narrator imagines what her father must have been like. Kincaid explains this in a recent interview in *Black Issues Book Review*: "*Mr. Potter* had to be fiction, because for one thing, I knew nothing about this man [my father]. I had only his birth certificate, his death certificate and his father's birth cer-tificate to go on. I didn't know anything about him except that he was a chauffeur."[15]

This estrangement from the father accounts for the angry tone of the narrative voice. In fact, the narrator's rage at the father she never knew is emotionally powerful and intense, even though it is mediated through a clear understanding that Mr. Potter was a product of forces that he could neither change nor understand. The narrator, for instance, recognizes that her father could not love his children because he never received enough love himself. As a child, he was left in the care of friends by his mother, who was never to return, and he was abandoned by his own father. Mr. Potter is, in turn, estranged from his own chil-dren, and the history of familial abandonment repeats itself. Such repetition is highlighted by Elaine, the narrator, but she also illustrates how this vicious cycle can be broken, for she refuses to repeat his mistakes. As such, she puts distance between herself and her father, referring to him as an illiterate man who could never fully understand his surroundings. By contrast, she describes herself as a lover of books, a prolific writer, and as someone who is devoted to her children. There is, then, a core of hope in this otherwise angry and bleak novel: the narrator implies that the cycle of history, the repetition of the past, can and will be broken.

The reviews of *Mr. Potter* have, in general, been positive. However, some reviewers were disappointed by the text. In the *Observer*, for example, Adam Mars-Jones writes that Kincaid's style is defined by "incantation and repetition," but that "nothing in *Mr. Potter* disproves the rule that incantation works best with children, congregations and juries."[16] Likewise, Andrew Roe writes in the *San Francisco Chronicle* that "*Mr. Potter*, with its circularity and tedium and repetition, nevertheless taxes even the most patient and open minded of readers. You can only read about the sun being in its usual place so many times."[17] And Maya Jaggi writes in the *Guardian* that the narrative voice includes a "vindictive" tone "that is sour and self-regarding."[18] The positive reviews of the novel have tended to focus on Kincaid's poetic use of language. Curdella Forbes, for instance, states that the language of the text is "stunning," "compelling," and "musical."[19] And Kim McLarin states that Kincaid's writing style in *Mr. Potter* is "rich, layered, lyrical, and often hypnotic."[20]

One of the things that has irritated some readers is the fact that *Mr. Potter* is largely plotless. It is, in short, a literary work without a main story, and the book does not move through a series of chronological events in a traditional narrative form. Instead tensions are offered up and never completely resolved. No attention is given to cause and effect: the moments of Mr. Potter's life are not arranged conveniently into plot points on a dramatic arc. And as the narrative moves from one thing to another, the narrator repeatedly states that the events have no meaning to the protagonist. As a result, the narrator often gives the details of Mr. Potter's absent thoughts and that which he "could not dwell on."[21] The prose thus captures a void in Mr. Potter, and the narrative deliberately undermines itself by negation. For each iteration highlights the distance between the unreflective, illiterate protagonist and the highly self-reflexive, literate voice of the narrator.

Although the story is skeletal and sparse, the language and syntax of the text are highly complex. What takes precedence, then, is the repetitive, stream of consciousness style of writing—a style that is foregrounded in the long first sentence of the novel: "And that day, the sun was in its usual place, up above and in the middle of the sky, and it shone in its usual way so harshly bright, making even the shadows pale, making even the shadows seek shelter; that day the sun was in its usual place, up above and in the middle of the sky, but Mr. Potter did not note this, so accustomed was he to this, the sun in its usual place, up above and in the middle of the sky; if the sun had not been in its usual place, that would have made a great big change in Mr. Potter's day, it would have meant rain, however briefly such a thing, rain, might fall, but it would have changed Mr. Potter's day, so used was he to the sun in its usual place, way up above and in the middle of the sky" (3).

This is a remarkable and extraordinary beginning to a novel. The syntactically charged opening sentence is not only overwhelming in its long and sprawling nature, but it also begins with the word "And." This word, "And," is of course a conjunction, indicating that something has come before it. After all, conjunctions are used to join together sentences, clauses, phrases, or words. The initial "And," then, is a way for Kincaid to indicate that the narrative is continuing on from something else. And the reader, progressing through the narrative, realizes that this conjunction begins most of the sentences of the novel, including the start of every chapter and almost every paragraph. This writing strategy suggests that the beginning is not necessarily the beginning, implying that something has always come before the opening clause.

There is a literary tradition that Kincaid is drawing on here. Her use of conjunctions is yet another example of her debt to modernism. Ernest Hemingway, for instance, was quite fond of using "and"; he would often build long sentences using this conjunction as a bridge between non sequiturs. Gertrude Stein, too, liked to use "and" as a way of cataloging items and developing a writing style based on the repetition of words and phrases. This Steinian technique is clearly seen in Kincaid's novel, for words and phrases (such as "the sun in its usual place," etc.) are echoed throughout the text. Indeed Kincaid's practice of repetition, restatement, and revision means that ideas and words are sometimes stated three different ways in the same sentence. At other times, a statement of fact in one section is complicated by further information in another section. The shift in a verb from one position to another and the highly complex arrangement of commas and semicolons allows Kincaid to accumulate multiple meanings and to invoke conflicting ideas. This writing style contributes to the fragmentary nature of the narrative by telling the life of Mr. Potter in a series of contradictory comments and incongruous circumstances. Thus Kincaid implies that the best way to tell the story of Mr. Potter is to avoid telling it. For the contradictions, incongruities, revisions, and repetitions demand the reader's unwavering attention: the writing of the story demands constant rewriting, and as a result, the reading of it also requires a continual rereading.

Mr. Potter shares many similarities with Kincaid's previous work. It is, like most of her fiction, set in Antigua and explores the stifling confinement of living in this small place. Moreover, the novel occasionally invokes political and historical perspectives, particularly when the narrator refers to the year 1492 as the year that marks the European conquest of the Caribbean. At the same time, though, the text does not only blame the arrival of Columbus and the colonization of the island as the only source of suffering in Antigua. The narrator also recognizes that all life includes a mixture of pleasure and pain: "The great cauldron of misery and small cup of joy that is all of life" is something that people everywhere must come to terms with (42). From this perspective, colonization and racism are invoked but also deconstructed as part of the more general suffering that affects all life.

Kincaid also inserts herself into the text. Once again she plays on the border separating fact from fiction, the real from the unreal. Self-referentiality is an important aspect of her writing style, and in *Mr. Potter* the narrator shares Kincaid's birthday and her birth name. In addition, many of the events in the narrator's life parallel Kincaid's own experiences, particularly when the narrator decides to escape Antigua by fleeing to New York. The writer and the narrator, then, are connected as they seek to create out of nothing a relationship with an unknown father: this accounts for the repetition and the endless variations on the sentence, "Mr. Potter was my father" (58).

Although the text focuses on the figure of the father, the narrator's mother occasionally flickers into life: "She [my mother] then was flames in her own fire, not waves in her own sea, she would be that later, after I was born and she had become a woman, she would become that to me, an ocean with its unpredictable waves and undertow; she was then flames in her own fire and was very beautiful" (135). This passionate and powerful image of the mother is contrasted to the passive and inert character of Mr. Potter. He has no control over his life, and he has no influence on those who surround him. He is neither loving, nor is he loved. In fact, for the narrator he is a blank page upon which she inscribes his life. And this leads to the statement that she is "the central figure in Mr. Potter's life," a proposition that can only be true on paper (48).

While earlier novels such as *Annie John* and *The Autobiography of My Mother* deal with the strained mother-daughter relationship, *Mr. Potter* centers on the bond between an estranged father and daughter. From this perspective, the narrator seeks to breathe new life into a distant man she never knew. Such an objective focuses on the desire to understand her own alienation and abandonment but also to try and comprehend his (and thus her) place in the universe. However, the image of the mother—a strong and passionate woman who is also estranged from her own father—hovers forever in the background of the text. But Annie's relationship to her father differs from that of Elaine's in that Annie has brought about this estrangement. Raised on the island of Dominica, Annie flees her home and moves to Antigua after a series of "violent quarrels" she has had with her father (118). This story parallels the real life of Kincaid's mother, a Dominican who moved to Antigua because of the tension between her and her father. It is not surprising, then, that Kincaid has identified her mother as being the main inspiration for writing *Mr. Potter*. "It [*Mr. Potter*] came to me in thinking about my mother," Kincaid states in a recent interview, "the more I thought of her life, and how it was that I grew up without knowing this person that she loathed and who was my father, the more I wanted to write this book. Here was a person she absolutely detested."[22]

From this anchor of fact and emotion, Kincaid creates Elaine, the autobiographical persona who imagines Mr. Potter's life with his fisherman father and absent mother. Throughout the narrative, Elaine reveals the hatred between her parents that has scarred her own life. She has been kept from Mr. Potter by an overprotective mother, and her father's profound dislike of Elaine's mother causes him to remain distant. Her anger, though, is generally directed at her father, and this becomes acute as she traces the cycle of deprivation and abandonment. (In fact, Mr. Potter has had eleven daughters with eight different women, all of whom he has abandoned.) Through the emotionally charged aspects of her life, Elaine pieces together a fragmentary portrait of her father, "whom history had made into nothing, a thing of no spiritual value" (178). Indeed as she describes his birth, life, and death in a narrative that purports to be his story, Elaine builds an indictment of her father's actions (his irresponsibility), and she condemns him for being unaware of the pain that he has caused others. Mr. Potter is, Elaine states, oblivious to the suffering of his abandoned women and children in "houses that had only one room and four windows" (120). Instead of acknowledging his responsibility, he walks through life singing, preening, and reserving his love for the cars he covets.

This portrait is completed by what Elaine sees as the most important fact of Mr. Potter's life: he was "born with a line drawn through him, for his father's name did not appear on his certificate of birth" (97). This fact is significant because it links Mr. Potter's life to Elaine's; she too has a line drawn through her, since her father did not likewise acknowledge her existence. This mark, this lack in Elaine's life, is addressed in her act of writing. That is, throughout her narrative, she seeks to heal herself through the cathartic and empowering process of telling her story. In so doing, she examines her father and expresses a desire to purge the paternal emptiness from her life by further understanding the man who was so central to her conception and life, but who was always a ghostly presence. Rage is one way that Elaine deals with this emptiness: "Mr. Potter did not have a uterus that shuddered in agony, for he was a man, and he did not have a menstrual cycle, for he was a man. . . . I never knew him at all, had never touched him, or known how he smelled after a night of sleep or after a full day's work" (136). Such a statement can be read as an externalization of anger that offers healing. Once this rage is expressed, Elaine can see the history behind her father's dereliction. Mr. Potter's lifetime, she states, "began in the year 1492," and it has unfolded in the shadow of an Anglican church built by his African slave ancestors (175–77). Colonial mimicry, she concludes, fuels his neglect of his family.

The consequences of history also affect the characters who surround Mr. Potter. For instance, his employer, Mr. Shoul, is from "the Lebanon or Syria, someplace like that, barren and old," while Dr. Weizenger, a Czech immigrant who was forced to flee Europe, is marked by his narrow escape from death in the Holocaust (6). Their experiences of oppression and war echo the colonial history that has marked Mr. Potter. And yet these men have no connection to each other; their circumstances do not allow them to know the histories that shadow each of their lives. The similarities in their lives can only be seen by Elaine, who states that they have all in some way been formed by the histories of "upheavals and displacements and murder and terror" that "could break the heart of an ordinary stone" (7). History, then, haunts the lives of the characters; they are not free from their pasts. But the narrative also suggests that the way to move forward in the present is to recognize common and shared histories. For the stories of the Syrian, the Jew, and the Antiguan all include their own savage plots—plots that need to be told in order for them to be understood. At the same time, though, *Mr. Potter* does not undertake to tell a lost story or rewrite history. Rather the narrator retains a skepticism about the possibility of discovering a hidden truth, and the novel reveals a consciousness troubled by such a notion of recovery or unquestioned truth. All the narrator can do is look at the consequences of history, make connections, and try not to repeat the mistakes of the past.

One of the reasons Mr. Potter cannot make connections to others is because he is not self-aware. Indeed, throughout the book Elaine comments on this lack and equates it with Potter's illiteracy. An inability to read, she suggests, contributes to his underdeveloped self-consciousness. She thus asserts that "because Mr. Potter could neither read nor write, he could not understand himself," and she goes on to say that "Mr. Potter did not own himself, he had no private thoughts" (90). Such an equation functions as an allegory in the text. Mr. Potter's inability to read, write, or understand himself casts him as a symbolic figure that leads to larger generalizations about human existence on this island. Consequently the narrative of *Mr. Potter* moves from the personal story of an imagined father to a more general and symbolic exploration of life on Antigua. In this transition, the conditions of Mr. Potter's life become representative of the conditions experienced by a large percentage of the population. The narrator, then, implies that Antigua is a country where the citizens are kept in ignorance. They are not encouraged to become literate or pursue education. They are not taught to be critical or to contemplate the meanings of their lives. And they are not inspired to connect their current situations (the fact that they do not own themselves) to a history of slavery and colonization.

Part of this symbolic move is captured in Mr. Potter's expression "Eh, eh." Throughout the novel, Elaine's father repeatedly expresses these two sounds that are not words or even syllables of words, but mere utterances. "Eh, eh," says Mr. Potter over and over again to himself, to his employers, and even to his daughter while dismissing her from his presence. This utterance sometimes marks the beginning of a declaration or the end of a statement. At other times it is used as an evaluation or an exclamation. Sometimes it expresses a question or an inquiry. And still at other times it is used as a dismissal or to express scorn and incredulity. The narrator does not always comment on the meaning of Mr. Potter's utterance, but she sometimes speculates that the expression means nothing at all, that her father is not capable of producing meaning in language.

Mr. Potter's "Eh, eh" is a refrain that suggests an expressive lack—a lack of language, a lack of self-awareness, and a lack of understanding. But it also lies in sharp contrast to the narrator's voice, which expresses complex ideas and celebrates the possibilities of language and articulation. Such a juxtaposition is clearly stated when Elaine reflects upon the death of Mr. Potter: "And Mr. Potter, like his father Nathaniel, could not read and neither of them could write, and their worlds, the one in which they lived and the one in which they existed, ceased, and the small, irregular stumble that their existence had made in the vast smoothness that was the turning of the earth on its axis was no more and was not celebrated or even regretted by anyone or anything. And from Mr. Potter I was made, and I can read and write and even love doing so" (55).

And yet at other times in the novel "Eh, eh" is joined to the narrator's prose when, on a few occasions, Mr. Potter's expression is restated in the voice of the narrator. An example of this occurs when Elaine writes that the "opening of all the windows by Mr. Potter made Mr. Potter look out at all the light outside, how it thrilled him ('E ah make me trimble up inside, 'e ah make me feel funny)" (19). Elaine's parenthetical offering recasts her description in Mr. Potter's own language. Such a revision and repetition speaks to the orality of Mr. Potter's life, for the sentence encourages the reader to speak his words aloud in order to clarify his communication and make meaning of his expressions. This style of writing intentionally scrambles the text on the page and suggests that for reasons of clarity and comprehension the words should not remain unspoken.

Some reviewers have suggested that in writing about her father in this way Kincaid appropriates her father's voice by not letting him speak. Maya Jaggi, for instance, asserts that the writing in *Mr. Potter* "becomes revenge" because the telling of her father's story is "a means of silencing him."[23] But such a claim overlooks the blankness of Mr. Potter. His expression, his empty "Eh, eh," and his blank mind are said to be full of nothing. From this perspective, it is important to view Mr. Potter as unable to speak for himself—he is at a loss for words—and, as a result, his daughter must speak for him. She thus fills in the blank space of his mind (a space that echoes the blank spaces on the birth certificates), by inscribing emotions, desires, and histories that he cannot articulate.

Notes

Chapter 1—Understanding Jamaica Kincaid

1. For more information on the literary awards won by Kincaid, see Ike Onwordi, "Wising Up," *Times Literary Supplement* (London), November 29, 1985, 13.

2. For more information on her life, including a "Jamaica Kincaid Chronology," see Jeremy Taylor, "Looking Back in Anger," *Caribbean Beat* 67 (July–August, 2005): 1–8.

3. Jamaica Kincaid, "Jamaica Kincaid's New York," *Rolling Stone*, October 6, 1977, 71.

4. Selwyn R. Cudjoe, "Jamaica Kincaid and the Modernist Project: An Interview," *Callaloo* 12, no. 2 (1989): 396–411. Reprinted in *Caribbean Women Writers: Essays from the First International Conference*, ed. Selwyn R. Cudjoe, 215–32 (Wellesley, Mass.: Calaloux Publications, 1990).

5. Kincaid discusses her change of name in an interview with Allan Vorda published in the *Mississippi Review* 20, no. 1 (1991): 7–26.

6. Doris Grumbach, quoted in Diane Simmons, *Jamaica Kincaid* (New York: Twayne, 1994), 18.

7. Susan Sontag, jacket for *At the Bottom of the River.*

8. Derek Walcott, quoted in Leslie Garis, "Through West Indian Eyes," *New York Times Magazine*, October 4, 1990, 80.

9. Paula Bonnell, *Boston Herald*, March 31, 1985, 26.

10. Susan Kenny, "Paradise with Snake," *New York Times Book Review*, April 7, 1985, 6.

11. Jacket copy for *Annie John.*

12. Donna Perry, "Jamaica Kincaid: An Interview," in *Backtalk: Women Writers Speak Out; Interviews with Donna Perry* (New Brunswick, N.J.: Rutgers University Press, 1993), 136–37.

13. Alison Friesinger Hill, "Jamaica Kincaid," *New York Times Book Review*, July 10, 1988, 19.

14. Adewale Maja-Pearce, "Corruption in the Caribbean," *New Statesman and Society,* October 7, 1988, 40.

15. Caryl Phillips, "Islands in the Dark: Review of Jamaica Kincaid's *A Small Place,*" *Los Angeles Times Book Review,* July 17, 1988, 12.

16. Salmon Rushdie, quoted in Simmons, *Jamaica Kincaid,* 19.

17. Jane Mendelsohn, "Leaving Home: Jamaica Kincaid's Voyage Round Her Mother," *Village Voice Literary Supplement,* October 1990, 21.

18. Both statements appear on the jacket cover of *Lucy.*

19. Margaria Fichtner, "'Mother' Is the Invention of Kincaid's Necessity," *Albany (N.Y.) Times Union,* January 14, 1996, 10.

20. Cathleen Schine, "A World as Cruel as Job's," *New York Times Book Review,* February 4, 1996, 2.

21. Peter Kurth, review of *My Brother, Salon,* October 9, 1997, http://www.salon.com/books/sneaks/1997/10/09reviews.html (accessed January 2007).

22. Meredith Maran, "*My Brother:* Book Review," *San Francisco Chronicle,* October 10, 1997, 12.

23. Kim McLarin, "An Interview with Jamaica Kincaid," *Black Issues Book Review,* July–August 2002, 7.

24. Jeremy Taylor, "Looking Back in Anger," *Caribbean Beat* 67 (July–August 2005): 6.

25. Adam Mars-Jones, review of Jamaica Kincaid's *Mr. Potter, Observer* (London), July 28, 2002, 25.

26. McLarin, "Interview with Jamaica Kincaid," 7.

27. The influence of modernism and early-twentieth-century literature on Kincaid is not surprising when we consider her comment in a recent interview: "I thought writing died at the beginning of the 20th-century, because all of the works I read as a child were from that time. I thought writing had gone out of fashion until I came to America and lived with a family, and the man was a writer. It was then that I realised people were still writing and that I might do it." See McLarin, "Interview with Jamaica Kincaid," 7.

28. Mars-Jones, review of Jamaica Kincaid's *Mr. Potter,* 25.

29. Some critics, such as Louis James, have suggested that Kincaid's writing does not fit into any of the fashionable schools of Caribbean writing. Other critics, such as Laura Niesen de Abruna and Helen Tiffin, see connections between Kincaid's fiction and the Caribbean writing of Jean Rhys and Erna Brodber.

30. McLarin, "Interview with Jamaica Kincaid," 7–8.

31. Quoted in Simmons, *Jamaica Kincaid,* 5.

Chapter 2—Early Stories

1. Edith Milton, "Making a Virtue of Diversity," *New York Times Book Review,* January 15, 1984, 22; Diane Simmons, *Jamaica Kincaid* (New York: Twayne, 1994), 73.

2. Jamaica Kincaid, *At the Bottom of the River,* 1st Aventura ed. (New York: Vintage, 1985), 3–5. Hereafter cited in the text.

3. Walcott's comment appears in Leslie Garis, "Through West Indian Eyes," *New York Times Magazine,* October 7, 1990, 80.

Chapter 3—Early Novels

1. Susan Kenncy, "Paradise with Snake," *New York Times Book Review,* April 7, 1985, 6.

2. Amy K. Levin, *Africanism and Authenticity in African-American Women's Novels* (Gainesville: University Press of Florida, 2003), 89; Babacar M'Baye, "Gendered Africanisms: New Perspectives on Black Women in Africa and in the Diaspora," http://www.h-net.org/reviews (accessed March 2004).

3. Jamaica Kincaid, *Annie John* (New York: Farrar, Straus and Giroux, 1985), 3, 130. Hereafter cited in the text.

4. Selwyn R. Cudjoe, "Jamaica Kincaid and the Modernist Project: An Interview," in *Caribbean Women Writers: Essays from the First International Conference,* ed. Selwyn R. Cudjoe (Wellesley, Mass.: Calaloux Publications, 1990), 220.

5. Diane Simmons, *Jamaica Kincaid* (New York: Twayne, 1994), 101.

6. See H. Adlai Murdoch, "Severing the (M)Other Connection: The Representation of Cultural Identity in Jamaica Kincaid's *Annie John,*" in *Jamaica Kincaid,* ed. Harold Bloom (Philadelphia: Chelsea House, 1998), 115.

7. Thulani Davis, "Girl-Child in a Foreign Land," *New York Times Book Review,* October 28, 1990, 6.

8. Jeremy Taylor, "Looking Back in Anger," *Caribbean Beat* 67 (July–August 2005): 6.

9. The Jamaica Kincaid special issue is *Callaloo* 25, no. 3 (2002): 780–989.

10. Gayatri Chakravorty Spivak, *A Critique of Postcolonial Reason: Toward a History of the Vanishing Present* (Cambridge: Harvard University Press, 1999), x.

11. Jamaica Kincaid, *Lucy* (New York: Farrar, Straus and Giroux, 1990), 6. Hereafter cited in the text.

12. For a thorough analysis of the name Enid, Lucy's desire to kill her mother, and the act of renaming, see Kristen Mahlis, "Gender and Exile: Jamaica Kincaid's *Lucy,*" *Modern Fiction Studies* 44, no. 1 (1998): 178. For an analysis of the name Enid in the context of the imperialist writing of Enid Blyton, see Moira Ferguson, *Colonialism and Gender from Mary Wollstonecraft to Jamaica Kincaid* (New York: Columbia University Press, 1993), 130.

Chapter 4—Nonfiction

1. Jamaica Kincaid, *A Small Place* (New York: Farrar, Straus and Giroux, 1988), 80. Hereafter cited in the text.

2. Alison Friesinger Hill, "Jamaica Kincaid," *New York Times Book Review,* July 10, 1988, 19.

3. Isabel Fonseca, "Their Island Story," *Times Literary Supplement* (London), January 13, 1989, 30.

4. Milca Esdaille, "*A Small Place:* Book Review," *Black Issues Book Review,* September 2000, 12.

5. Diane Simmons, *Jamaica Kincaid* (New York: Twayne, 1994), 136.

6. Allan Vorda, "Interview with Jamaica Kincaid," *Mississippi Review* 20, no. 1 (1991): 19.

7. For the financial information on Barclays Bank, see James Anyanzwa, "Big Banks, Big Trouble," *Financial Standard,* August 17, 2005, 5. For more information on the GNP for Antigua and Barbuda, see the United Nations Statistics Division, Department of Economic and Social Affairs, http://unstats.un.org/unsd/snaama/ (accessed April 2006).

8. *Life and Debt,* directed by Stephanie Black, Tuff Gong Pictures, 2001. This film is a feature-length documentary that addresses the impact of the Inter-American Development Bank, the International Monetary Fund, and current globalization policies on developing countries such as Jamaica.

9. Diane Hartman, review of *My Brother, Denver Post,* December 7, 1997, 5.

10. John Skow, review of My Brother, *Time,* November 10, 1997, 108.

11. Anna Quindlen, "The Past Is Another Country," *New York Times,* October 19, 1997, 23.

12. Sarah Kerr, "The Dying of the Light," *Slate,* October 21, 1997, http://www.slate.com/id/3018 (accessed January 2007).

13. Marilyn Snell, "Jamaica Kincaid Hates Happy Endings," *Mother Jones,* September–October 1997, 28.

14. Jamaica Kincaid, *My Brother* (New York: Farrar, Straus and Giroux, 1997), 75. Hereafter cited in the text.

15. Quindlen, "The Past Is Another Country," 23.

16. Kathleen M. Balutansky, "On Gardening: An Interview with Jamaica Kincaid," *Callaloo* 25, no. 3 (2002): 799.

17. Jamaica Kincaid, "In History," *Callaloo* 20, no. 1 (1997): 1–7.

18. Jamaica Kincaid, *My Garden (Book)* (New York: Farrar, Straus and Giroux, 1999).

19. Kincaid's texts on gardening also include the volume she edited titled *My Favorite Plant: Writers and Gardeners on Plants They Love* (New York: Farrar, Straus and Giroux, 1998), as well as *Among*

Flowers: A Walk in the Himalaya (New York: National Geographic Books, 2005).

Chapter 5—Recent Novels

1. Margaria Fichtner, "Jamaica Kincaid's *Autobiography of My Mother,*" *Miami Herald,* March 17, 1996, 14.

2. Paul Grondahl, "Pouring Her Soul into Her Words," *Albany (N.Y.) Times Union,* February 13, 1996, 5.

3. Grondahl, "Pouring Her Soul into Her Words," 5.

4. Rosellen Brown, *The Autobiography of My Mother* (New York: Dell, 1976), 246.

5. Moira Ferguson, "A Lot of Memory: An Interview with Jamaica Kincaid," *Kenyon Review* 16, no. 1 (1994): 175.

6. Ibid., 176.

7. For more on this, see Donna Perry, "Jamaica Kincaid: An Interview," in *Backtalk: Women Writers Speak Out; Interviews with Donna Perry* (New Brunswick, N.J.: Rutgers University Press, 1993), 129.

8. Leslie Garis, "Through West Indian Eyes," *New York Times Magazine,* October 4, 1990, 80.

9. Derek Walcott, "A Far Cry from Africa," in *Collected Poems, 1948–1984* (New York: Farrar, Straus and Giroux, 1986), 17–18.

10. Burt Schneider, "Geography Lessons: An Interview with Jamaica Kincaid," *Hungry Mind Review* 1 (Winter 1997): 8.

11. Jamaica Kincaid, *The Autobiography of My Mother* (New York: Plume, 1997), 3. Hereafter cited in the text.

12. However, the Caribs were able to retain some islands, including Dominica, St. Vincent, St. Lucia, and Trinidad. In fact, Carib resistance delayed the European colonization of Dominica, and the Carib communities that remained in St. Vincent and Dominica retained a degree of autonomy well into the nineteenth century. But the last known speakers of the Island Carib language died in the 1920s, and the number of Caribs in Dominica today is approximately three thousand. For more on the history of the Carib people,

see Samuel M. Wilson, ed., *The Indigenous People of the Caribbean* (Gainesville: University Press of Florida, 1998), 180–85.

13. Gerhard Dilger, "I Use a Cut and Slash Policy of Writing: Jamaica Kincaid Talks to Gerhard Dilger," *Wasafiri* 16 (1992): 23.

14. Dwight Garner, "Jamaica Kincaid," *Salon*, November 8, 1995, http://www.salon.com/05/features/kincaid.html (accessed January 2007).

15. Kim McLarin, "An Interview with Jamaica Kincaid," *Black Issues Book Review*, July–August 2002, 7–8.

16. Adam Mars-Jones, review of Jamaica Kincaid's *Mr. Potter*, *Observer* (London), July 28, 2002, 19.

17. Andrew Roe, "The Tics of Kincaid's Prose Fill the Mind of *Mr. Potter*," *San Francisco Chronicle*, May 19, 2002, 18.

18. Maya Jaggi, "Bitter Fruit," *Guardian* (Manchester), August 3, 2002, 12.

19. Curdella Forbes, "Writing the Autobiography of My Father," *Small Axe* 7, no. 1 (2003): 173.

20. Kim McLarin, "*Mr. Potter*: Book Review," *Black Issues Book Review*, July–August 2002, 9.

21. Jamaica Kincaid, *Mr. Potter* (New York: Knopf, 2002), 7. Hereafter cited in the text.

22. McLarin, "An Interview with Jamaica Kincaid," 7–8.

23. Jaggi, "Bitter Fruit," 12.

Selected Bibliography

Books by Jamaica Kincaid

Among Flowers: A Walk in the Himalaya. New York: National Geographic Books, 2005.

Annie John. New York: Farrar, Straus and Giroux, 1985; London: Picador, 1985.

At the Bottom of the River. New York: Farrar, Straus and Giroux, 1983; London: Pan, 1984.

The Autobiography of My Mother. New York: Farrar, Straus and Giroux, 1996; London: Vintage, 1996.

Lucy. New York: Farrar, Straus and Giroux, 1990; London: Cape, 1991.

Mr. Potter. New York: Farrar, Straus and Giroux, 2002; London: Chatto & Windus, 2002.

My Brother. New York: Farrar, Straus and Giroux, 1997; London: Vintage, 1998.

My Favorite Tool. New York: Farrar Straus and Giroux, forthcoming.

My Garden (Book). New York: Farrar, Straus and Giroux, 1999; London: Vintage, 2000.

A Small Place. New York: Farrar, Straus and Giroux, 1988; London: Virago, 1988.

Talk Stories. New York: Farrar, Straus and Giroux, 2001; London: Vintage, 2001.

Books Edited by Jamaica Kincaid

The Best American Essays 1995. Boston: Houghton Mifflin, 1995.

The Best American Travel Writing 2005. Boston: Houghton Mifflin, 2005.

My Favorite Plant: Writers and Gardeners on Plants They Love. New York: Farrar, Straus and Giroux, 1998.

Selected Interviews with Jamaica Kincaid

Balutansky, Kathleen M. "On Gardening: An Interview with Jamaica Kincaid." *Callaloo* 25, no. 3 (2002): 790–800.

Cudjoe, Selwyn R. "Jamaica Kincaid and the Modernist Project: An Interview." *Callaloo* 12, no. 2 (1989): 396–411. Reprinted in *Caribbean Women Writers: Essays from the First International Conference.* Edited by Selwyn J. Cudjoe, 215–32. Wellesley, Mass.: Calaloux Publications, 1990.

Dilger, Gerhard. "I Use a Cut and Slash Policy of Writing: Jamaica Kincaid Talks to Gerhard Dilger." *Wasafiri* 16 (1992): 21–25.

Ferguson, Moira. "A Lot of Memory: An Interview with Jamaica Kincaid." *Kenyon Review* 16, no. 1 (1994): 163–88.

Garner, Dwight. "Jamaica Kincaid." *Salon,* November 8, 1995, http://www.salon.com/05/features/kincaid.html (accessed January 2007).

McLarin, Kim. "An Interview with Jamaica Kincaid." *Black Issues Book Review,* July–August 2002, 7–8.

Mendelsohn, Jane. "Leaving Home: Jamaica Kincaid's Voyage Round Her Mother." *Village Voice Literary Supplement,* October 1990, 21.

Perry, Donna. "Jamaica Kincaid: An Interview." In *Backtalk: Women Writers Speak Out; Interviews with Donna Perry,* 127–141. New Brunswick, N.J.: Rutgers University Press, 1993.

Schine, Cathleen. "A World as Cruel as Job's." *New York Times Book Review,* February 4, 1996, 2.

Schneider, Burt. "Geography Lessons: An Interview with Jamaica Kincaid." *Hungry Mind Review* 1 (Winter 1997): 8–9.

Taylor, Jeremy. "Looking Back in Anger." *Caribbean Beat* 67 (July–August 2005): 1–8.

Vorda, Allan. "An Interview with Jamaica Kincaid." *Mississippi Review* 20, no. 1 (1991): 7–26.

Selected Books about Jamaica Kincaid

Bloom, Harold, ed. *Jamaica Kincaid*. Philadelphia: Chelsea House, 1998. This academic treatment of Kincaid's work includes important essays from international scholars working on Kincaid.

Bouson, J. Brooks. *Jamaica Kincaid: Writing Memory, Writing Back to the Mother*. Albany: State University of New York Press, 2005. This book draws on autobiographical sources to argue that Kincaid uses her writing to transform her feelings of shame into pride by constructing a positive personal and political identity through her texts.

Burrows, Victoria. *Whiteness and Trauma: The Mother-Daughter Knot in the Fiction of Jean Rhys, Jamaica Kincaid and Toni Morrison*. London: Palgrave, 2004. This study combines close reading, contextualization, and cultural theory to focus on issues of race and contemporary theorizing of whiteness and trauma in Kincaid's depictions of the mother-daughter relationship.

Covi, Giovanna. *Jamaica Kincaid's Prismatic Subjects: Making Sense of Being in the World*. London: Mango Publishing, 2004. This is an examination of Kincaid's contribution to feminist and post-colonial theories over the past 20 years. The relevance of Kincaid's writing is demonstrated through its capability to account for contemporary sociocultural complexities and point the way toward a politics of collective justice.

Ferguson, Moira. *Jamaica Kincaid: Where the Land Meets the Body*. Charlottesville: University Press of Virginia, 1994. This highly political study offers an energized exploration of imperialism in Kincaid's work and suggests that the theme of colonization is developed through deflection and indirection.

Paravisini-Gebert, Lizabeth. *Jamaica Kincaid: A Critical Companion*. Westport, Conn.: Greenwood, 1999. This companion to Kincaid's work offers much biographical information, but few strong literary analyses of Kincaid's texts.

Simmons, Diane. *Jamaica Kincaid*. New York: Twayne, 1994. This introduction to Kincaid's work offers biographical information alongside clear critical examinations.

Stanton, Katherine. *Cosmopolitan Fictions: Ethics, Politics, and Global Change in the Works of Kazuo Ishiguro, Michael Ondaatje, Jamaica Kincaid, and J. M. Coetzee*. New York: Routledge, 2005. This unique academic and highly theoretical study argues that *My Brother* is part of a genre of global literature that investigates the ethics and politics of complex and multiple belonging.

Selected Articles about Jamaica Kincaid

Anatol, Giselle Liza. "Speaking in (M)other Tongues: The Role of Language in Jamaica Kincaid's *The Autobiography of My Mother*." *Callaloo* 25, no. 3 (2002): 938–53. This is a scholarly essay that offers a strong reading of the role of languages (English, French, and Creole) in the complicated mother-daughter relationship.

Broeck, Sabine. "When Light Becomes White: Reading Enlightenment through Jamaica Kincaid's Writing." *Callaloo* 25, no. 3 (2002): 821–43. This complex essay looks at Kincaid's depiction of "whiteness" in the context of Enlightenment thinkers such as John Locke and white supremacists such as Josiah Nott and Arthur de Gobineau.

James, Louis. "Reflections and the Bottom of the River: The Transformation of Caribbean Experience in the Fiction of Jamaica Kincaid." *Wasafiri* (Winter 1988–1989): 10–15. This scholarly article examines questions of illusion and reality in Kincaid's early fiction.

Lima, Maria Helena. "Imaginary Homelands in Jamaica Kincaid's Narratives of Development." *Callaloo* 25, no. 3 (2002): 857–67. This lucid essay focuses on *Lucy* and *My Brother* to explore Kincaid's representations of home and diaspora in the context of personal and national identities.

Mahlis, Kristen. "Gender and Exile: Jamaica Kincaid's *Lucy*." *Modern Fiction Studies* 44, no. 1 (1998): 164–83. This scholarly article argues that *Lucy* challenges the masculinist conventions of traditional exile narratives.

Scott, Helen. "'Dem tief, dem a dam tief': Jamaica Kincaid's Literature of Protest." *Callaloo* 25, no. 3 (2002): 977–89. This is an academic essay examining *A Small Place, Lucy,* and *My Brother* as works that expose the legacy of colonization and new forms of domination in the Americas.

Smith, Ian. "Misusing Colonial Intertexts: Jamaica Kincaid, Wordsworth and Colonialism's 'Absent Things.'" *Callaloo* 25, no. 3 (2002): 801–20. This scholarly examination of *Annie John* and *Lucy* places the novels in relation to the English literary canon.

Index